MW00677797

I Can Appreciate That

Replacing negative space with the hidden blessings of challenge

a memoir of gratitude by

STEVEN CRANE

Copyright © 2021 Steven R. Crane

All rights reserved.

ISBN: 978-0-9965987-2-9

FOR:

My parents, Bob and Nola Crane - the strongest people, and best teachers, I know.

My wife, Carie - the greatest Appreciator in my life.

My boys, Matt & Liam - wise and kind beyond their years. How excited I am for everything you have yet to Appreciate.

With sincere thanks and gratitude to:

Carie, Jeff, Angela, Madison, & Greta

Your time and talents have Appreciated this work significantly.

Credits:

Cover design: Jeff Quigley

Illustration: kjpargeter / Freepik.com

Author photo: Greta Zefo

I CAN APPRECIATE THAT

Contents

Introduction

Perhaps the thing I like and appreciate most about this book is its timing. The idea for this journey happened in the early fall of 2019. By that winter, I had already begun outlining and putting down the first real words. By the time we were into the first few months of 2020 and were starting to realize that this would be a year unlike any other most of us had ever seen or experienced, I was already firmly committed to this project. 2020 progressed, and by many peoples' accounts, continued to *regress* in terms of our enjoyment of the year. But my writing continued. As you might imagine, in any long writing project, the author gets immersed in their subject matter. Even when not actively *writing*, your subject is a constant companion, as you're either thinking about what you just wrote or organizing your thoughts and preparing for the next chapter. So, what happens when your subject matters are gratitude and appreciation? Good things happen, at least to your brain and your heart. Like all of us throughout 2020, I've had my share of conversations with family, friends, and colleagues about how everything "sucks" and how I can't wait to get back to "normal" to visit friends, travel, see live music, etc.

But not surprisingly, this frustration was tangibly tempered by this project, especially when I had the opportunity to share what I've been working on with a friend. In fact, I often described the process of thinking about and writing these essays as "marinating my brain in gratitude" for a year. For a self-described pessimistic cynic, that was probably a good idea in general. In this particular year, though, consistent time with these ideas of gratitude and appreciation had a remarkable, positive effect.

In many ways, I need to be grateful for and appreciative of 2020 itself, not for the hardships and suffering it has brought to so many I know, and to countless others worldwide, but for the unique opportunities it has created. 2020 has been unkind to many in the context of employment or health, for example. I am eternally grateful for the opportunities I have had this year to continue practicing my craft as a professional writer and for the relationships that have created those opportunities. I also recognize, ironically, it was the disappearance of some of my paying jobs that existed before the pandemic that gave me time and space for this project. I might have found time to do this writing anyway, but my mindset, and thus the end product, would have been different.

It's as if something beyond me was inviting me to spend that time and energy elsewhere, to share what I've learned as I prayed about and reflected on these crucial concepts of gratitude and appreciation. In that regard, the words and stories contained here are products of a specific moment in time. But I also hope their ultimate message is somewhat universal and timeless. Regardless of the season of life we find ourselves in, whether it be a time of drought and doubt or a year of great bounty and success, there is always room, and a genuine need, for gratitude and appreciation.

I don't know when you will encounter these words, but I hope you will embrace the simple truths revealed to me through this year of marinating in appreciation. My prayer for you is that they bring you as much insight and comfort as they have me, now and ever forward.

"Don't forget, a person's greatest emotional need is to feel appreciated." – H. Jackson Brown Jr.

Setting the Table

It may sound counterintuitive based on this book's title, but I should probably admit right up front that I am cynical; a real "glass is half empty" kind of guy. That might even be too kind. A lot of the time, I can be downright pessimistic. For various reasons (some known to me and others perhaps not), I've often tended to see what's wrong in a situation first. I know this about myself and have become more honest about it – both with others and myself – as I have gotten older. At points in my life, I've even worn the title of curmudgeon like a badge, calling myself a "realist" and scoffing at my more joyful brethren as people who just hadn't experienced enough hardship to lose some of that obnoxious perpetual optimism.

Being the cynical guy can be okay. It becomes part of your identity, a role you play in group dynamics, etc. Sometimes it gives – like when a well-timed, dry-witted joke hits the mark and everyone laughs. But probably more often than not, it takes.

Recently, I had an epiphany courtesy of one of the smartest, most observant, and most honest people I know. That person happens to be my teenage son, Matt. We were having a discussion – about what exactly, I can't even recall. But in the course of that conversation, he stopped me cold, replying to my statement with a striking charge I'll never forget. His words to me were, "Dad, why are you always so negative about everything?"

Sometimes, the feedback we receive from others is easily disregarded or deflected. And sometimes, the sheer weight and honesty of a critique are enough to crush your soul. He was right, and the truth hurt.

And that's where this exercise was born. In one statement, my son abruptly opened my eyes and forced me to not only consider the question he asked but also to think hard about why my perspective is what it is. And more importantly, could I change?

I know from personal experience that it is possible to change how one feels or thinks – about people, events, issues, etc. As I near 50, I know with certainty there are things I see and think about differently than when I was 15, 25, or 40. But what about your entire outlook? Is it possible to change the fundamental way we think about things or the actions that come from those thoughts? I decided to try and find out.

Like so many other aspects of human nature, both nature and nurture influence our world view. Some studies show direct correlations between a person's genetic makeup and their propensity for positivity – suggesting that optimism is partly genetic. And yet, as author B.J. Neblett would tell us:

"We are the sum total of our experiences. Those experiences – be they positive or negative – make us the person we are at any given point in our lives. And, like a flowing river, those same experiences, and those yet to come, continue to influence and reshape the person we are and the person we become. None of us are the same as we were yesterday, nor will be tomorrow."

The truth is likely a combination of both, but as Neblett suggests, we do have the potential to change, evolve and improve. That gives me hope for myself and all of us.

Defining "Appreciate"

In the interest of maybe finding some answers, let's start with a question: What's the first thing you think or say to yourself when things go wrong?

When something unideal or unfortunate happens to you, how often do you find yourself thinking, *"I don't appreciate that?"* For me, it happens *all* the time. It could be something small, even trivial, like when someone cuts you off in traffic or sneaks in and grabs that great parking spot right before you. Or it could be something much more significant, like learning you didn't get that particular job, or when you or someone you care about has a truly existential crisis with health, finances, or relationships.

When I say, "I don't appreciate that.", I can situationally mean several different things. On an emotional level, it translates to, "That makes me (mad, sad, frustrated, etc.)," or "That hurts me." From a more rational perspective, it's merely a replacement for "I don't like that."

So, what does it mean to "appreciate" something? It depends.

As you'll come to see in these pages, I distinguish between "appreciation" and "Appreciation." The former almost always refers to a singular act or instance of valuing an experience. As I'll explain in greater detail in a moment, the latter refers to a larger concept - the one at the heart of this book.

The word "appreciate" has several unique definitions, four of which form the foundation for this exercise. Individually, they all have value. When combined and thought of as an ascending process, that value increases exponentially. As a baseline, let's look at each definition in detail:

ap·pre·ci·ate

to understand fully; recognize the full implications of.

"They could appreciate the pressure he was under."

synonyms: acknowledge, recognize, realize, know

This definition might not be the first meaning of the word that most of us would arrive at, but it probably is the best place to start.

Perhaps you're familiar with 12-step programs – the ones designed to aid in recovery from addiction, compulsion, or other behavioral issues. Among these programs' foundational tenets is: "The first step to solving a problem is admitting you have one." To take action and do anything with a situation (whether it be an opportunity or an obstacle), we must first be aware of, recognize, and acknowledge it.

This first definition of "appreciate" is critical. Advocates and alumni of those 12-step programs will tell you that progress through the rest of the process isn't possible without the first step of acknowledgment. Often, that first step can be the most difficult though because it requires us to have some degree of faith in an outcome usually beyond our current horizon. Here, Hebrews 11:6 would caution, but also encourage, us that *"Without faith, it is impossible to please Him, for whoever would draw near to God must believe that He exists and the He rewards those who seek Him."*

Our approach to Appreciation should be similar. We must faithfully pursue our destination, secure in the belief that great rewards await, even if the road that takes us there is hard to see.

And to be clear, I don't want to minimize the act of acknowledgment; it is essential. But for this exercise, this first definition of "appreciate" is perhaps the one that requires the least of us. It's one thing to recognize we have a problem or an opportunity. But most often, what comes next – the WHAT and HOW of doing something about it – is much more challenging work.

This is pretty basic, but it's just the on-ramp to the highway that leads to our ultimate destination. Here's the next step:

ap·pre·ci·ate

recognize the full worth of.

"She feels he truly appreciates her"

synonyms: value, respect, prize, cherish, treasure

This second definition of "appreciate" builds on the first and adds more context. Only after we realize and acknowledge that something exists can we recognize its full value. This recognition takes an extra level of awareness and a little more work. Before we can "think highly" of something or someone, we must first actually THINK about it or them. For something to gain respect or value, we must spend some time considering it in the context of our own beliefs or values. And "spend" probably isn't even the right word. It's more like "invest." Recognizing the FULL worth of something

6

requires an investment on our part, above and beyond, just acknowledging that it merely exists.

Now, we're getting somewhere. But we're only halfway to where we want to be. Here's the next definition:

ap·pre·ci·ate

to be grateful for (something).

"I would appreciate any information you could give me."

synonyms: be thankful for, be obliged or indebted to

Once we have acknowledged something and invested a little time recognizing the value it holds, it's possible to reach the next level of Appreciation. Just like before, this definition builds on the others and requires even more from us. That next step is GRATITUDE. This is where appreciation moves from being mostly informational to more *transactional* and where it really starts to gain the power to become *transformational*.

If your understanding of gratitude is simply being grateful or giving thanks, you are correct. But if you stop right there, you might be missing something essential. Another part of the definition of gratitude is "to be indebted to." This is the *transactional* part. If someone gives you something of value, you are accountable to, or indebted to, the giver. Sometimes this is simple and straightforward. If someone lends you money, you would be obliged to repay them both morally and legally. But what about other things of value? When someone, whether friend, stranger or even adversary, blesses us with kindness, are we not likewise indebted to repay this as well?

When God blesses us (with gifts or opportunities), He does so freely because He loves us. We are supposed to receive those gifts with gratitude, too – with thanksgiving and a desire to reciprocate that love. Look at Psalm 126:3. *"The Lord has done great things for us. We are glad."* And the directive in 1 Thessalonians 5:18 that we should *"Give thanks, all the time."*

7

So how do we repay God? He, and His store of blessings, is infinite. There is nothing God needs from us at all. But that doesn't mean we have nothing of value to GIVE in that relationship.

For the answer to how we can genuinely repay our blessings, we turn to the final definition:

ap·pre·ci·ate

to rise in value or price.

"They expected the house to appreciate in value."

synonyms: increase, gain, grow, rise, inflate, escalate

The first three definitions of "appreciate" – to understand, to recognize, and to be grateful for (our blessings) – have the power to change *our* lives. Just knowing good things have and will continue to come to us brings a feeling of peace and well-being. It also helps fill our cups in preparation to weather life's storms. But there's something more. The last definition of "appreciate" has an even greater power: the power to change OTHERS' lives, and thus the world around us.

We just spoke about appreciation being "transactional." This typically means there is a "give/get" dynamic at work between two entities. The first three definitions of "appreciate" are all about us GETTING. First, we gain an understanding. Then, we realize or recognize the value of that knowledge. Then, ideally, we get a feeling of gratification from the blessings we have received. In all of that, we GET a whole lot. So, what about giving?

The final definition of "appreciate" is about "increasing value," which is where the transaction gets completed. Here, we are taking what we are given and GROWING it. This definition most often gets applied to financial or other tangible assets. Over time, your house or your stock portfolio will likely appreciate. That is, wisely invested, it will grow in value. This growth enriches our lives, allows us to better care for our families and others, and generally empowers us to make positive changes in the world around us. The same should be true of our blessings as well.

Think of it this way: in every instance, the word "appreciate" takes the form of a verb. Traditionally, this means it is a word that "does work." Fully realized, Appreciation (as a concept and a process) requires us to be the actors – the ones who do the work.

If we're living in full Appreciation, we're not content to just *understand* and *recognize* that we GOT something good. *Thanksgiving* for these blessings is a crucial elevation of appreciation, but even that isn't quite enough.

In Jeremiah 30:19, we're told, *"From them will proceed thanksgiving and the voice of those who celebrate; And I will multiply them, and they will not be diminished; I will also honor them, and they will not be insignificant."*

God wants our blessings to be *multiplied*. But how? Sometimes it is by His grace alone. For our part, though, multiplying the gifts we have received is about investing what we receive and sharing what we've gained (and learned). That is how we create greater value – for ourselves and others. That is the real power of Appreciation.

From appreciate to Appreciate

So, that's the bigger picture of Appreciation as a concept. As a person who loves words and uses them daily in my work, I can say that I was already aware of these four definitions. But I had never really thought about them together as a progressive path – not until my son inadvertently invited me to do so. His one simple question – "Dad, why are you always so negative?" – unlocked a door for me. When I opened it, I found a literal lifetime of memories and experiences that probably deserved to be revisited and reconsidered.

And, so, here we are. If my original, cynical perspective leads me instinctively to proclaim, "I don't appreciate that," this book is my journey of walking toward a different understanding. What follows in the chapters ahead is my attempt to understand how that mindset was formed and begin the process of filling that negative space with a new truth.

It's easy enough to appreciate the good things in our lives. But what about the not-so-great stuff? Matt's invitation to me, and ultimately mine to you, is about finding the blessings we've missed along the way – the ones hiding in our biggest challenges, frustrations, or perceived failures. I'm confident if I think about it the right way, surely, I Can Appreciate That.

Understanding How "I Can Appreciate That"

Now that we have our definitions for "appreciate," let's put them to work. For this exercise, it helps to boil them down even further. Here is a simple framework, or series of filters, through which we can view any situation in order to fully "Appreciate" it.

Step 1: Acknowledgement = **"I See It"**

Step 2: Understanding = **"I Get It"**

Step 3: Thanksgiving = **"I'm Grateful"**

Step 4: Increasing Value = **"I'll Grow What I Got"**

Each of the essays in this collection follows this basic framework. In some, the Step 4 dividends from the original investment are obvious. In others, they may be more subtle, but still very much there. In either case, the process above helped create real change in my thoughts about specific experiences and my overall perspective.

In hindsight, I recognize walking through these steps invited me to look at the events covered in these stories comprehensively – considering my perspective before, during, and after. Looking forward, I'm encouraged by the possibility of Appreciation becoming a constant, "in the moment" mindset – more of a way of life for the present and future than a tool for reflecting on the past.

We could stop right here, and you would have gotten basically what you need to apply the Appreciation process to your own life and thinking. But, let me invite you to keep walking with me. I have a few stories to tell you.

- Before reading the definitions provided here, how would you define the word "appreciate?"

- Have you already started thinking about what you might (and might not) appreciate in your own life?
  - What blessings am I misinterpreting as challenges or curses?
  - What am I missing altogether?

- What am I UNDER-appreciating? (What do I SEE but not GET, GET but not value, or value but not increase in value?)

- What can I say I have fully Appreciated?

Wisdom to Appreciate:

(Existence)
Hebrews 11:6 – And without faith, it is impossible to please Him, for whoever would draw near to God must believe that He exists, and that He rewards those who seek Him.

(Recognition)
"The first step in solving a problem is to recognize that it does exist." – Zig Ziglar

(Thanksgiving)
Psalm 126:3 – The Lord has done great things for us. We are glad.

1 Thessalonians 5:18 – Give thanks, all the time.

(Investment)
Jeremiah 30:19 – From them will proceed thanksgiving and the voice of those who celebrate; And I will multiply them and they will not be diminished; I will also honor them and they will not be insignificant.

Prologue: How We Got Here

A cynical mind might question God's plans or intent, or even His very presence or existence in the face of difficulties, obstacles, and tragedies. A more faithful spirit rests in the certainty that God doesn't make mistakes and finds solace in knowing that while we might not always know, understand, or agree with His Plan for our lives, surely He is making all things work together for our good.

In episodes from my own life, several experiences pop out as prime candidates for re-examination. We'll get to those in due time. First, though, a quick detour. I want to start by sharing a tale that demonstrates the awesome power of Appreciation, and which doesn't involve me at all.

An Unlikely Story

There is a semi-famous writer/director named Kevin Smith. I say "semi-famous" because depending on how old you are, what kind of lifestyle you live, and what you find funny or interesting, you might not have encountered his work or even know who he is. On the other hand, for a specific portion of the population (mostly middle-aged men who like crass humor, comic books, and weed), Kevin Smith is a bit of a cultural icon. Based on the potentially dubious description I just gave of him, he also might seem an unlikely candidate for a position on my Mount Rushmore of gratitude and appreciation, but stick with me for a minute.

In 1994, Smith released his debut film *Clerks*, which he shot in black and white on a shoestring budget of just $27,575 in the same

New Jersey convenience store where Smith had once worked. *Clerks* would go on to make a relatively impressive $3 million at the box office and effectively launch Smith's career, which to date includes having written or directed 15 films and numerous television episodes and commercials. In 2019, *Clerks* was selected by the National Film Registry for preservation in the U.S. Library of Congress due to its "cultural, historical, and aesthetic significance." In the 25 years between its release and this honor, Smith has cultivated a near cult-like following of loving fans who continue to appreciate and show uncommonly strong support for the artist and his work.

I saw *Clerks* when it first came out. I was 22 years old and squarely in the target demographic. I remember liking it, but not in a way that particularly stuck with me. It was just another movie I had seen. I'd go on to see many of Smith's other films, viewing them in more or less the same way – enjoying them at the moment and then moving on. It wasn't until much later that I would gain a whole new appreciation for Kevin Smith as a creative force in specific, and a human being in general. That's because Kevin Smith is a central figure in one of the most compelling gratitude stories I know.

Remember that pack of rabidly loyal Kevin Smith fans I mentioned? I've come to learn that there are a surprising number of people who take their love for Kevin and his work to extremes. There are multiple communities online dedicated to discussing his movies and characters. There are hordes of people who travel to film, television, and comic book conventions worldwide to see Kevin and others like him speak about their creations. And there are even people who spend their free time and energy creating their own artistic interpretations and homages to Kevin Smith's work. All of this – even cosplay and fan fiction - is semi-standard in the celebrity-obsessed world in which we live. The internet is drowning in celebrity shrines, most of which go unrecognized, and probably even unseen, by the actual famous people they celebrate.

Mr. Smith appears to have a different approach, one that is much more interactive and seems to be deeply rooted in a spirit of gratitude.

In full disclosure, I don't know Kevin Smith personally. I have met him twice and spoken to him for a minute or so each time – likely engaging in some version of the same basic awkward conversation famous people have when they meet plain, non-famous people like me. But what I do know is that Kevin Smith knows how to Appreciate people and their gifts because I've seen it happen.

I Need You to Know, What You Do Matters to Me

Let me introduce you to the other main character in this particular story. For more than a decade, I worked as a writer in a global advertising company's Atlanta office. There, I had many creative partners – among the finest of whom was a lovely man named Jeff. At the time, Jeff was an artist living in a small, remote town on Canada's Eastern shore. Perhaps the most telling and endearing of Jeff's qualities is his passion. If he cares about something (a project, a person, a cause, etc.), there is no length to which Jeff won't go to ensure the right things happen. In this regard, Jeff is a near-perfect articulation of the urging we get in 1 Corinthians 16:14 to *"Let all that you do be done in love."*, which at least from my distant perspective seems fitting of Kevin as well.

In the twenty years Jeff and I have been friends, I have seen and benefitted from this love and dedication countless times. My world is a better place because Jeff is in it, and for that, I am eternally grateful.

Whereas I was a casual fan of Kevin Smith, Jeff was decidedly more passionate. In 2012, Kevin was doing a roadshow, traveling to different cities to meet fans and tell stories with one of his long-time collaborators, producer Scott Mosier. When that show came to nearby Halifax, Jeff decided he needed to make something – a piece of fan art – as both a commemorative gift and a thank you. It turned out to be a large movie-type poster featuring Kevin drawn in Jeff's uniquely awesome illustrative style.

Jeff managed to get his poster sent backstage at that show, and to his delight, it was returned to him, signed by both Kevin and Scott. The story could have ended right there, and Jeff would have been happy enough.

As he had done countless times before, Jeff shared his work online. And, as was typically the case, he received plenty of positive feedback from friends, family, and even perfect strangers. This piece was destined for bigger things, though. Jeff's poster caught the eye of a then-random stranger named Jim, who was already partnering with Kevin. Jim was working to provide custom jerseys for one of Smith's pet-projects – the View Askew Street Hockey League, a collection of 16 amateur street hockey teams competing in and around Ontario, Canada.

Enamored by Jeff's work, Jim reached out and asked Jeff to develop new logos and jersey crest designs for the teams. As an art director, illustrator, and graphic designer, Jeff had already done volumes of logos, including playing around with designs for various hockey jerseys. If you know Kevin Smith, you know he has spent a good portion of his adult life dressing exclusively in a uniform consisting of jean shorts and hockey jerseys. So, it's not surprising that eventually, Kevin himself would see Jeff's work in this format. Around the same time, Jeff developed another piece of fan art (a parody presenting Kevin's face in the style of Colonel Sanders of KFC fame). Kevin saw this piece and liked it so much, he personally reached out and asked to use the artwork on a custom jersey for his wardrobe.

Again, the story could end right there, and Jeff would have exceeded his own expectations – getting closer than he probably ever imagined to an artist he appreciated and respected. But that's not even close to the end.

Now Kevin had SEEN Jeff's work. But he hadn't just SEEN it; he GOT it and liked it too. Not only did Kevin like it, but he also recognized its value (both creatively and its spirit of appreciation). So, what did Kevin Smith do? Kevin decided to truly Appreciate Jeff's talent by increasing its "value" exponentially.

Remember, Kevin Smith and other famous people get presented with things like this frequently. Most of these shows of fan appreciation garner little attention and create even less consequence. From the very beginning, Kevin could have done NOTHING at all. He could have let the poster come and go. The jersey designs for VASHL? Jim and Kevin could have thanked Jeff for the efforts and went on their way, having themselves also benefited from Jeff's passion and talent.

Kevin had other ideas, though. And from there, the flood gates opened. After delivering that first custom crest, Jeff continued to get requests directly from Kevin. Whenever an idea would hit him – often early in the mornings, California-time – Jeff would get texts from Kevin asking if he could design another crest. Soon enough, Jeff had created a whole closet's worth of custom hockey jerseys for Kevin, which were getting seen by vast numbers of people as he wore them to show tapings, live performances, and public appearances. Not a bad return on the investment of time and passion Jeff had made in creating that first poster. Wait. It gets better.

A few years later, Kevin was preparing to launch a new film, *Yoga Hosers*. Teasers started showing up on various social platforms, and once again, Jeff was inspired. Again, he created a custom illustration – this time of characters from the film, and posted it online, tagging Kevin. A few days later – the day after Christmas – Jeff gets a text from Kevin with another request. The ask? Illustrating an entire comic book to tell the back-story (which Kevin hadn't even written yet) of the film as a promotion for its debut at the Sundance Film Festival. Oh, and he needed it in FIVE days!

Of course, it would mean burning a ton of midnight oil, after full shifts at his day job and taking care of other family responsibilities. But what an opportunity! Again, Kevin could have just thanked him and paid him for the work. In the end, though, Jeff wound up flying to Aspen, Colorado, and attending the film's debut at Sundance – a Bucket List experience for sure.

That's a storybook ending whose proportions and origins are both righteously Biblical. Consider 1 Peter 4:10 – *"Each of you should use whatever gift you have received to serve others, as faithful stewards of God's grace in its various forms."* That's precisely what Jeff did. In Kevin's response, look at Proverbs 22:29 – *"Do you see someone skilled in their work? They will serve before kings; they will not serve before officials of low rank."*

So, how does all of that happen? Gratitude. Jeff appreciated what Kevin did so much that he invested his time and talent to send him a custom piece of art. In turn, Kevin appreciated Jeff's gesture so much that he went beyond creating a single memorable, personal interaction and instead started a multi-year relationship that wound up exposing Jeff's artwork to a global audience he might never have realized otherwise. All because one person took the time to appreciate someone else – to say, *"Hey, what you do is cool. Here's what I do."*

This story is extraordinary but not unique. I've seen enough of Kevin's other speeches and gestures to know that this spirit of appreciation is an underlying current in his basic makeup as a person. He frequently reminds audiences that while he's getting to live his dream, there's absolutely NO reason the rest of us can't do the same thing. He's also quick to encourage people to share their ideas and remind people to ask for help in bringing them to life. That's the kind of stuff that can sound like lip service unless you've seen the speaker literally put his money where his mouth is.

Why did I start a book about appreciation with a story about Kevin Smith? It's a good story, for starters, but it also perfectly demonstrates the full cycle of Appreciation. It also illustrates a powerful point. Even though that story doesn't involve me at all, it still gave me the chance to look outside myself and see the power of Appreciation at work in someone else's life. Getting to see people you care about experience joy and be rewarded for living in gratitude; that's a gift unto itself.

See It. Get It. Be Grateful. Grow It. These are the constant markers on this journey. You'll find them repeatedly in the stories of my life – and hopefully, start recognizing them in your own.

Questions to Consider:

- What's your best story of gratitude that doesn't involve you personally?

- Take the time to think that story all the way through in terms of the full Appreciation cycle? How might your appreciation for the people and results of that story change once you do?

- Have you had the blessing of being able to share that story, either with the people involved or others, and express your gratitude?

Wisdom to Appreciate:

Proverbs 22:29 - Do you see someone skilled in their work? They will serve before kings; they will not serve before officials of low rank.

1 Peter 4:10 - Each of you should use whatever gift you have received to serve others, as faithful stewards of God's grace in its various forms.

Romans 12:6 - Having gifts that differ according to the grace given to us, let us use them: if prophecy, in proportion to our faith.

1 Corinthians 16:14 – Let all that you do be done in love.

Chapter 1:
Meet the Family

To come full circle, if you haven't seen Kevin Smith's movie *Clerks*, you should. The film centers on a character named Dante Hicks, who, while lamenting the many inconveniences he encounters during an unscheduled day at work, continually reminds us: "I'm not even supposed to be here today!"

Me neither, Dante; me neither.

Every person has a unique heritage story, full of intriguing twists and turns that somehow result in each of us being born. I don't for a minute think that my story is any more interesting, valuable, or important than anyone else's. But when I think about all the crazy things – some completely unforeseen that are matters of seconds or inches – that had to happen in precisely the right sequence, I know it's truly remarkable that the collection of cells known as me even exists.

Or is it? Jeremiah 29:11 is pretty specific. *"For I know the plans I have for you, declares the Lord, plans for welfare and not for evil, to give you a future and a hope."*

Perhaps what's even more amazing is to consider the happenstances that bring us to our current place in time as part of such a grand, forethought, Master Plan. I still may not know exactly *why*, but at least here's *how* I got here.

The Patriarch: A Matter of Life and Death

My great-grandfather, Giuseppe Ciammaichella was born in 1884 in Chieti – a small town in eastern Italy, near the Adriatic Sea and about 120 miles from Rome. Obviously, I never met him, and sadly I only have a patchwork of details from his life – but what a story they tell.

As a young man, in addition to being a husband and father of three children, Giuseppe had the distinction of serving in the Carabineri – the Italian military police and the fourth branch of the Italian Armed Forces. The name "Carabineri" comes from the French, meaning "soldier, with a carbine." Appointed as armed escort-protectors of the sovereign, these soldiers could realistically expect to see plenty of action and danger.

In 1912, at the age of 28, Giuseppe's life turned on a dime. While in the active service of King Victor Emmanuel III, he was personally responsible for the death of two Mafioso members. That's the kind of event that draws mixed reactions. I'm sure there were those (the Italian government, his colleagues, and his family) who were pleased with this outcome. I'm also sure the Mafia felt quite differently. At that point, Giuseppe had two options – stay in Italy, as a marked man with a potentially short shelf-life or flee.

My great-grandfather immigrated from Italy to the United States in 1912. He arrived at Ellis Island alone (having only enough money for his own travel) and unable to speak a single word of English. He made his way to the Cleveland, Ohio area. Settling there, he would work tirelessly for the next two years until he had enough money to arrange passage to America for his wife and their three kids. He would never return to Italy.

Dissatisfied with the limited opportunities he found as an Italian immigrant (mostly as laborers and landscapers), Giuseppe Ciammaichella started his own enterprise with family members, a nursery business he would work at and grow for the rest of his life. He also grew his family.

The Hero

My grandfather, Joseph Henry Cimmaichella, was born in 1922, the first of three more children my great-grandparents would have in America.

In 1933, Giuseppe was involved in a serious car accident. At this time, the steering columns of many vehicles were still made of wood. The impact of the crash snapped the wheel, and the sheared post impaled Giuseppe's chest. He suffered a punctured lung but miraculously survived. Remarkably, he stayed in a hospital for only three days before returning to work. Less surprisingly, he never fully recovered. Giuseppe Ciammaichella died in 1934. My grandfather, Joseph, was 12 years old.

So, in 1934, in the middle of the Great Depression, and nestled directly between two World Wars, my grandfather was the pre-teen son of a widow, with two younger siblings, one of which had special needs after suffering brain damage due to the use of forceps during his birth. That last sentence alone is enough to give me great context, and great appreciation, for the relative ease with which I live today.

Joseph's father, Giuseppe, saw segregation and discrimination limiting the opportunities of Italian immigrants and quickly learned English to improve his prospects. Forbidden by Giuseppe to speak Italian even in their own home, Joseph and the rest of his family would learn too. This quest to escape cultural discrimination would play another pivotal role in my eventual future, but we'll get to that in a minute.

As a child, my grandfather was an accomplished violin player and the only musician in the family. His fully realized talent was a testament to his parents, who recognized and nurtured it, even given the cost amid the realities of the Great Depression. From this early age, Joseph was already playing in organized orchestras alongside adults. He would play regularly at local events and parties, often in bars and taverns. This exposure to night club life gave him several valuable insights. One such lesson was a front-row seat for "appreciating" what alcohol did to people. As a 12-year-old, he had the wisdom to process that and decide that alcohol would never really be part of his life.

A few years later, Joseph approached a crossroads – one of those moments where your life either goes down one path or another depending on the outcome. The orchestra he was playing with had secured an audition at Radio City Music Hall in New York City. The lead vocalist of their group had a terrible cold the day of the audition, and even though the instrumentalists were well received, the group failed the audition. I assume success that day would have sent him in a vastly different direction, but that "failure" sent Joseph back to Cleveland.

On December 7th, 1941, the Japanese attacked Pearl Harbor, catapulting the United States into World War II. My grandfather enlisted immediately, joining the U.S. Army Air Corps with the intent of becoming a pilot. For various reasons, that didn't happen. He washed out of pilot training but remained part of the Air Corps, where his technical and engineering aptitudes landed him as Chief Technician and turret gunner on a B-17 crew based in England. In this role, he wasn't there to fly the planes. He was there to fix them (not if, but) when they broke or got damaged during flight. And if the pilot and co-pilot became incapacitated during a mission, it was his duty to land the plane. I don't know if he ever had to do that, but I know for sure this is well beyond the requirements of any job I've ever had.

In 1942, at the age of 19, Joseph Ciammaichella began joining active bombing raids over Germany. Over the next three years, he would fly the full complement of 36 bombing missions. Let me put that in context. In a single raid in 1943, 376 B-17s were deployed. Sixty of them were shot down, resulting in the death of over 600 crew, a 16% loss rate. Even if that far exceeded the average, which it doesn't, it means that it was almost statistically impossible to survive even 25 bombing missions, let alone 36. The odds of me even being here just got considerably longer.

Having completed his full tour requirement, Joseph got a new assignment. In May of 1945, the war ended, and my grandfather returned home with two Purple Hearts for combat injuries and quite a few stories. He was 23.

Remember my mentioning my great-grandfather's concern over cultural discrimination? A couple of decades and a Herculean contribution by Italian-Americans to America's victorious war effort didn't fix that issue. Upon his return from Europe, my grandfather encountered much of the same treatment. Not wanting his opportunities to be limited, he made a bold decision in response. In April of 1947, Joseph legally changed his last name from Ciammaichella to Crane – taking the new moniker from one he had seen on plumbing fixtures. He made this decision separate from his siblings, and as such, there are still several Ciammaichellas living in America today, mostly in the suburbs of Cleveland. In doing so, Joseph Henry Crane became the patriarch of an entirely new branch of a family tree planted centuries ago in Italy. My grandmother would bring Irish roots, to which English ancestry would be added a generation later through my mom's side of the family.

One evening, in late 1945, Joseph Ciammaichella joined a fellow veteran and good friend of his on a double-blind date. That night, he met a young lady named Betty Daugherty. Just a few months later, on July 20th, 1946, they married. In May of 1947, my grandparents would welcome their only child, my father, Robert Henry Crane.

Already, you can see a pattern forming. My great-grandfather and grandfather both encountered several significant, potentially life-altering (or even life-ending) events. Again, I know that all of us have these pivotal moments in our histories – places where if one small thing happens just a little differently, or not at all, everything changes. None of those stories make me special in any way, but they do offer a unique opportunity to consider and truly appreciate what could have been – or more pointedly, what could NOT have been.

Just seeing it is one thing, and a fun trip down Memory Lane for sure. But when you step back, take a closer look, and start recognizing the bigger arc you exist on, it gives you a greater appreciation for the sacrifices that precede you. These struggles had to be endured and overcome for you even to have a chance to exist. Already, I've reached a level of gratitude for those sacrifices that increases my appreciation for my forefathers. That leaves me wondering what I can do to ultimately Appreciate their contributions and increase the value of what they gave me. And, I haven't even told you about my dad yet.

The MVP

My father was born in Cleveland, Ohio, in 1947, becoming the first person in our family to arrive under the new name of Crane. Him even being here today was similarly unlikely, and not just because of the events outlined above. His mother, my grandma Betty, had been diagnosed with epilepsy. Because she was prone to grand mal seizures and other related symptoms, she was already under medical supervision. When she became pregnant soon after their marriage, the doctors frankly advised her that it would be best for her health if she did not complete the pregnancy. Had she listened to that advice, the Crane branch of the Ciammaichella family tree would have sprouted, withered, and died all in one single generation – and I wouldn't be here today.

Joe and Betty did NOT listen to that advice, and, on May 29th, 1947, they welcomed Robert Henry Crane into the world. Betty's health stabilized, but only temporarily. In 1952, after more complications, she needed major surgery to address multiple lesions on her brain. We've come a long way, in a lot of ways, since 1952. Brain surgery is not among the least of these. The procedure, which my dad describes as having similar results to a partial lobotomy, saved her life, but she was never the same.

So, by the age of five, my dad was cooking, cleaning, doing laundry, and taking care of his mother, while his dad was working hard to support their family. My dad's father was a committed, loving parent and dove in hard. He became my dad's baseball coach and his Scout Master in the Boys Scouts to make sure they had quality time together. He coached until my dad reached a level that exceeded his ability to help any further and then hung up his cleats. Boys Scouts was different. Even after his own son finished scouting, my grandfather continued to serve other kids in the community. Years later, he would earn the organization's Silver Beaver award for "distinguished service that has impacted the lives of youth." Those last few details don't have much to do with me being or not being here, but they help paint a clearer picture of the strong heart of service my grandfather had and would help instill in future generations of our family.

My dad had his own brush with disaster early in childhood. When he was eight, he nearly changed the course of our history in a freak kitchen accident. His mother had been cooking that day. She had used the deep fryer and then placed it atop a cabinet, with the cord wrapped around the handle of one of the doors on their stove-refrigerator combo. She'd also been baking cookies. When my dad opened the oven door, the deep fryer came flying down, covering him and the kitchen floor in grease. Fortunately, the oil had cooled sufficiently. If he'd have gone to get a cookie 30 minutes earlier, he'd have ended up with third-degree burns across the majority of his body. This accident probably wouldn't have ended his life, but it certainly would have changed it and erased the path that got me here.

That path, and the remarkable string of unlikely events that results in me, runs through the baseball field.

From an early age, my father played and loved baseball. The game has been one of his lifelong passions. As I write this, he is 73 years old and still playing on and coaching softball teams within his 55+ community – often playing quite competitively with some guys nearly two decades younger.

Like many of us, Bob started in Little League. Unlike most of us, he kept going. He was a standout pitcher on his high school teams, playing as a freshman with the varsity kids, and eventually earning a baseball scholarship to Western Michigan University.

Before heading to Kalamazoo for college, in the summer of 1965, my dad represented Collinwood High School on a Cleveland-area summer all-star team. Also on that team, another young pitcher from nearby Euclid, OH, named Steve Stone.

Stone would eventually play 11 seasons in the Major Leagues, pitching for the San Francisco Giants, Chicago's White Sox and Cubs, and the Baltimore Orioles. Steve Stone won 100+ games and the 1980 Cy Young Award as the best pitcher in the American League. Steve Stone was one of two MLB-caliber pitchers on that all-star team that won the city league championship in the summer of '65.

Bob Crane also had his sights set on making it to The Show, an entirely realistic goal. After a couple of years at Western Michigan, Bob had already caught the eye of at least one Major League club. In between seasons, a scout for the Philadelphia Phillies suggested he could get Bob a signing bonus to secure his services for that organization – another crossroads moment for sure. Stay in school, or take a modest payday and a shorter path to his desired goal? Either way, the decision would affect everything that followed. Ultimately, Bob consulted his dad. Together, they decided the bonus was less than the value of his scholarship at Western Michigan, so he went back to the Broncos.

Even though he may have foregone a potential short cut, Bob's master plan was still moving along as he imagined, and surely a future in professional baseball was on the horizon. Except, it wasn't.

In 1968, Bob Crane was a junior at Western Michigan University pursuing a degree in math (with designs to be a math teacher as his back-up plan). In preparation for another season of Broncos baseball, he took the field to pitch some batting practice to his teammates. Today, it's standard to have a netted L-screen in front of the pitcher to protect them from balls being batted back up the middle. On this day, there was no L-screen.

One of Bob's teammates, a hard-hitting third baseman named Eric Munther, stepped into the batter's box. Bob threw the ball, and before he even knew what had happened, it came screaming right back at him. That baseball hit Bob Crane square in the pitching hand, breaking several bones and effectively ending his baseball career on the spot.

Welcome back to the crossroads, where all your well-thought-out, well-intentioned plans meet fate and reality. Bob found himself with new choices to make. Baseball was over, in one cruel flash. What was next? Student teaching had ironically taught Bob that being a math teacher wasn't really what he wanted to do. So now what?

Bob made a radical choice – one that would shape, and continue to make possible, the rest of this story. No longer on scholarship, Bob Crane left Western Michigan University before graduating, returned to Cleveland, and started selling Ware-Ever® cookware. Among the tried-and-true tactics the company used was setting up displays in crowded public places where sales associates could catch potential customers' eyes and ears.

On what began as just another random day, Bob held one such demonstration at a local shopping mall. His target customers were young females, presumably ones who were either already cooking for families or would be soon. One such prospect allowed Bob to make his sales pitch. Some would tell you good salesmen are essentially "selling themselves" to customers. Bob was a student of this school. He somehow managed to talk this young lady into allowing him to demonstrate the quality of his cookware by offering to cook her dinner one night. As a testament to how different the world must have been in 1968, that customer accepted his offer. That customer was Nola Louise Beyer – my mom.

That first date went pretty well. In January of 1969, less than six months from the day they met at random in a shopping mall, Bob and Nola would marry. Just eleven months later, my sister, Kim, was born. I would follow two years after that, but only because...

1)   My great-grandfather killed two Mafiosi in the line of duty, escaped to America, and managed to bring his wife and children here two years later

2)   My grandfather defied all odds, surviving 36 bombing raids in WWII

3)   My father got injured in a freak accident, forcing him to choose a whole new life path

A baseball is three inches in circumference, and no matter what anyone tells you, it is pretty hard to hit, even in batting practice. If ANYTHING about the delivery of that one pitch had been different, or if Eric Munther had simply not swung his bat at it, I wouldn't be here. When you add that to the list of remarkable events in my grandfather and great-grandfather's lives, the outcome becomes even more unlikely. Or is "unlikely" even the right word?

And that lays bare the bigger picture behind all of this. One of two things must be true. Is the world, and our arc in it, the result of a series of random acts of unpredictable, uncontrollable chaos? Or, is there some sort of Master Plan, pulling us toward a preconceived end, in which God makes all things work together for the greater good, whether we see, understand, or appreciate it or not? I'll be honest. I've considered and embraced both viewpoints at various times in my life, not always being sure which is more likely or comforting.

In either case, I can say that when I think about all the crazy things that had to happen, the events that had to stack up and align just as they have, for me to be alive here and now... I feel compelled to try to Appreciate all of it. I've marveled at *seeing* that arc laid out for me in one continuous timeline. I've enjoyed the conversations with my family that helped me better understand those histories and helped me *get* it as I saw the bigger picture come into focus. And I've come to *recognize* the value of my predecessors' difficult choices and the results they generated. Now, it's my challenge to find a way to GROW what I've been given – through my own story and family. With two sons of my own, it's my responsibility to find a way to live in a way that honors my forefathers' investment, and God willing, somehow increases its value.

On that note, I circle all the way back to Kevin Smith, or more accurately, his character Dante Hicks. It's easy to look at the events of my family history and conclude that "I'm not even supposed to be here today." From there, it's right back to the crossroads. I AM here, so now what? Now, I get a chance to revisit the obstacles and opportunities I've seen in my own life, and with a renewed sense of purpose and optimism, genuinely decide: I Can Appreciate That.

Questions to Consider:

How did YOU get here?

• How well do you know the quirky twists and turns of your parents' and grandparents' lives?

• How unlikely must it be that everything in your family's history lined up JUST SO for you to be here right now?

• Does considering those odds make you less or more likely to appreciate your present blessings and future opportunities?

Wisdom to Appreciate:

Jeremiah 29:11 - "For I know the plans I have for you, declares the Lord, plans for welfare and not for evil, to give you a future and a hope."

Romans 8:28 – "And we know that all things work together for good to them that love God, to them who are called according to his purpose."

Chapter 2:
The Battle of Body and Mind

I just finished telling you about my family, and in the process, made the point that while my family history might be interesting, it's not necessarily unique. Most people have a few great stories about their ancestors. The next piece of my story is different though. These are experiences I suspect, and quite honestly hope, most of you *won't* have had. For better or worse, they are part of my journey though, and are things I can and should still try to Appreciate.

I was born on February 12, 1972, in Youngstown, Ohio, an arrival bringing both joy and great concern for my parents. You see, I was born with spina bifida, a birth defect caused when the neural tube (the structure that eventually becomes a person's brain and spinal cord) doesn't form correctly. There are several types of spina bifida, which range in severity depending on the size and location of the defect. My version, myelomeningocele (or open spina bifida) is the most severe type, wherein the spinal canal is open along several vertebrae in the lower or middle back. This results in the membranes and spinal nerves pushing through the opening at birth, forming an exposed sac of nerves and tissues on the baby's back. This condition makes the baby prone to life-threatening infections and may also cause paralysis and bladder and bowel dysfunction.

Typically, the first treatment for this condition involves a surgery to securely close the nerve sac. The procedure is life-saving but doesn't necessarily resolve the problem, and can often have permanent impact on the affected nerves and the parts of the body to which they correspond.

From the moment I arrived, I was sort of a literal representation of the half-full glass. On one hand, though my condition was severe, I was fortunate to have a relatively mild case. Many people born with open spina bifida never walk, are unable to have children, and require lifelong care for a variety of related complications. So, right from the start, I can appreciate that while my climb might be uphill, I am fortunate to have a chance at a relatively *normal* life. I inflect the word "normal" intentionally here, as my understanding of this concept would play a huge role in the person I would ultimately become and the lessons I would come to Appreciate from my experience.

On the other hand, practically speaking, my mom and dad were immediately faced with decisions no parent would envy. Neonatal medicine has advanced remarkably in the last 50 years. In 1972, my parents had no advance warning of my condition and were left to make those decisions in real time – a prospect I'm sure they didn't appreciate. The first in a very long line of those decisions was the initial surgery to close my spine. Left unrepaired, the fluid in the spinal sac would have traveled to my brain, causing encephalitis, and near certain death. On face value, it seems there wasn't much of a decision to make – or was there? From day one, my parents were given a choice. They could have decided, all things considered, with the many challenges I was sure to face, the easiest and maybe most compassionate thing to do would be to spare me – and themselves – those hardships by letting me pass. Or, they could resolve to love the blessing God had bestowed upon them and start walking down the difficult, uncertain path laid before them in the form of a special needs child. The fact you're reading this makes clear the choice they made, but it also provides the ultimate context for the rest of the stories you'll encounter here, and the nearly half century of blessings I've had the fortune to Appreciate as a result.

So, surgery it was, and a bit of a wait-and-see proposition in terms of what the future would bring. I would stay in the hospital for a week, recovering in the NICU and getting daily visits from my mom, whose interaction with me was limited to holding my hand through the walls of an incubator.

To add another level of stress, my parents, along with my 2-year-old sister, were in the process of moving from Canton to Youngstown when I was born. So, the place I came *home* to was actually the house of their best friends at the time. I should also mention, my dad was 25 and my mom was 23. I know "times have changed" and all that, but I include it as context for just how full my parents' plates were at a fairly young age. By comparison, my first child – one of two beautiful, healthy sons we would have – was born when I was 33 years old. I was nowhere near ready to manage even the basics of childcare – let alone for a child with a host of medical challenges – when I was 25. On that level alone, I have to appreciate my parents' strength and resolve.

As I prepared to write this, I reached out to my parents for help. I, of course, knew most of the big picture of my own health history, but many of the small details – especially those that occurred in my earliest childhood years just weren't there. In the notes my mom sent me, she mentions that after bringing me home and getting settled into a routine, "everything was pretty much *normal* for about the next year." There's that word again. What she meant was that it wasn't until I reached the age where I was supposed to be able to start walking that they realized I wasn't developing normally. In hindsight, as I look through her notes and think through my own memories, this cycle repeats itself time and again. In many ways, standard milestones of early childhood development – at least in a physical sense – became constant reminders for my parents that things were most certainly not "normal." In my youngest years, I had no real understanding of this reality. As I grew older though, this concept of normalcy, and the increasing realization that I was "different," became part of how I saw, thought of, and understood myself. There's plenty to unpack, and ultimately to Appreciate, there.

At the age of one, it was noticing my left foot was fused at an angle which made it impossible to walk without tripping. Finding it easier to drag myself with my arms than to walk in barred shoes, I developed broad shoulders, and the nickname "Bruiser." The physique and the moniker remain to this day. At two-and-a-half, it was the realization that, like many with spina bifida, my bladder wouldn't grow or function normally. By four, it was starting kindergarten with braces on my legs. At six, it was a surgery to straighten my crooked foot that succeeded, but led to a bone infection, another long hospitalization, and a year using crutches. At eight, it was the discovery of orthopedic shoes and custom orthotics as I attempted to join the *normal* kids playing baseball and soccer. There's more of course, but it's important to pause here for a second.

My youngest years were full of surprises. They also created plenty of instances where my parents were forced to make decisions for me based only on the information they had, the advice they got, and their gut assessment of what they thought would be best for me. That challenge alone isn't unique. Making choices for our kids is a challenge that befalls all parents. But clearly, some decisions are more complicated and consequential than others. I should take this, and every other opportunity I get, to say my parents did an amazing job here. And not just in making the hard choices that didn't always have obvious answers, but also in managing my frustrations through what seemed like a constant wave of no-win situations.

As a child, I spent plenty of time being angry. Aside from dealing with physical challenges, I caught more than my share of teasing from kids who could see I was different, but didn't understand why. I also suffered a good bit of bullying from others who identified me as the weak target. Usually, my anger from those experiences would spill onto my parents, with me looking to blame anyone I could for my situation.

Not that I truly questioned my parents' wisdom, but often, I thought things like *'If it would have been up to me, I would have made a different/better choice. I don't appreciate not getting to decide what happens to me.'* Here, "I don't appreciate that" actually means "I want to control something, but I can't, and that makes me mad as hell." Obviously, this anger was way more about my conditions themselves than about my freedom to make decisions related to them, but I wasn't able to see or understand that at the time.

It's also a thoroughly unfair exercise. It's always easier to question someone else's decisions than it is to make them ourselves. But second-guessing is a fool's game. Nothing productive or positive comes from that – unless it's context and appreciation for how hard someone else's position is.

In the moment, all you can do is take everything you know, have clarity on WHY you're making the choice you are, and then proceed with faith. My parents were tested countless times on this front, and though I might not have fully appreciated the choices they made in real time, I absolutely do now.

So, I'm an angry pre-teen who wants to make some decisions. Guess how that turns out. You know the old adage, 'be careful what you wish for, you just might get it'? Exactly.

Around the age of 12, one of the choices I made was to go outside and play without wearing shoes. That's about as simple and mindless a choice a kid can make, right? Not necessarily for a kid with spina bifida. You see, as a result of this condition – and as a product of that first surgery I had at two days old – I have very little nerve action, and thus severely decreased sensation below the knees. I can't really feel much of anything in or on my feet. So, it turns out that walking around in the yard barefoot that day was a really dumb decision – and one that would affect the rest of my life. At some point, I stepped on a small stone, the initial impact of which I never felt. That stone stuck to my foot, cut it, and began to work itself inside – all without my even noticing it. It wasn't until a couple of days later, as I was lying on the floor of our family room watching television, that my mom noticed a spot on my right heel. When she checked it, there was a ½" crater in my heel, into which that stone had burrowed itself – and I still never felt it. Back to the doctor we went. Amazingly, the stone, once extracted, more resembled a pearl than the pebble I had stepped on. Less surprising, I had managed to develop another infection. Worse still, because of its location, the infection had spread quickly through the soft skin to the nearest dense tissue – my right heel bone. Bone infections are serious stuff and very difficult to treat. And maybe the worst possible place to develop one would be on the bottom of one's foot, where every step creates additional trauma and interrupts the body's need for rest to heal.

Like the ripples that form from throwing a stone into a calm lake, the simple act of walking through my own yard barefoot would create a series of events that would echo for the rest of my life. Several more surgeries followed, along with my introduction to hyperbaric chamber therapy – a true joy for anyone who is even remotely claustrophobic. The goal of that treatment was to maximize oxygenation and blood flow to the area, to aid in healing. But spina bifida had left my feet and legs under-developed. A normal human foot and ankle has a total of 29 muscles. I only have about 12 of those, which was not enough native muscle to receive that healing blood flow. So, they borrowed a muscle from my back and transplanted it into my foot. That worked, sort of, but ultimately, they couldn't get the infection to clear. After multiple attempts to heal the affected area failed, doctors determined that cutting out the infected piece of bone was the only option remaining. As a result of that one decision, I earned myself a handful of additional surgeries, several weeks in the hospital, many more months on crutches, and lifetime of wearing orthopedic shoes, now further modified to account for my right leg suddenly being ½" shorter. I also would almost never walk barefoot again. I genuinely don't appreciate most of that. To this day, I get mad at myself and wonder how much pain I could have saved myself by wearing shoes that day – but even here there are hidden blessings.

As a father raising two teenage sons, I now watch my boys as they explore life – sometimes making decisions I know are less than wise. Probably too often, I interject, exhibiting the same protective instincts my own parents did. My sons don't have spina bifida – a fact for which I thank God every day. But they'll face plenty of other things as they navigate growing up in this complicated world. I can speak from experience on the powerful, lasting consequences simple choices make in one's life, and hopefully provide guidance that they'll benefit from and ultimately Appreciate themselves.

One thing my parents were always good at was trying to bolster my self-esteem. Most parents are mindful of this, as providing praise and reinforcement alongside discipline and guidance is generally a good recipe for producing decent humans. But my parents were particularly intentional in one regard. They did an excellent job of giving me realistic expectations. I mean this in multiple senses. They raised me to understand that I was *different*, but not *special*. By this, I mean they wanted me to know that while there were going to be things I would inevitably discover that I couldn't do, it didn't mean I shouldn't try. They also drew specific distinctions around areas of ability, reminding me fairly often that while I might have physical deficits, God had balanced the books by blessing me with a more-than-capable mind. My reality wasn't that I wouldn't have opportunities because of disabilities, it was that if I was intentional about applying the talents I did have, there was no reason I couldn't do anything I wanted. There's a confidence that comes from people believing in you, which when fostered consistently ultimately leads us to believe in ourselves. That's priceless, and appreciable. I'm trying hard to pay that same power forward to my own children.

It's Your Life; You Decide

Previously, I shared an example of how I wasn't always ready to make decisions for myself relative to my health. And there's grace enough in that; I was fairly young. My parents deserve massive credit for the degree to which they helped prepare me for the time when eventually, those decisions *would* be mine. And that time was coming.

In 1987, I was 15 years old. In many ways, I had the same thoughts, hopes, worries, and anxieties as anyone of that age. In other ways, my experience was completely different. Adolescence is complicated for everyone – even the most *normal* of kids. By the time I entered high school, I had spent nearly 10 years of my life surrounded by the same kids who, since first grade, knew me as "the kid who walks funny," "the kid in a wheelchair," "the kid who smells bad," "the kid on crutches." You get the idea. When you're five, the other kids see you're different, and their lack of understanding creates fear – they stay away. When you're ten, they still don't understand, but they make up stories and names to explain your situation to themselves and each other. After that, they start recognizing and feeling their own anxieties – the ways in which, in their own minds, *they're* "not normal." That's when they start lashing out, usually with words, and sometimes with fists.

By the time I was 15, I was pretty tired of that. I knew there wasn't much I could do to change the perception of people who had already "known" me for a decade. But I was trying hard to look past all that. If I could just make it a couple more years, I could move on – figuratively and literally – to college; to another place, where nobody knew me or my history. At the very least, I could restart the process of hiding all my baggage from the rest of the world, but with a clean slate. But, what if I had less baggage to actually hide? What if by some miracle, there was a way I could somehow *become* more "normal?" In the spring of 1988, that miracle arrived.

I mentioned that one of the effects of spina bifida was that my original bladder never fully formed. As a result, for my entire life up to that point, I had what is called an ileal conduit – a piece of small bowel drawn through the skin, attached to an external pouch to collect urine. I could describe this, and its associated complications, in great detail, but I imagine the physical, psychological, and social ramifications of going through one's formative school years as the kid with a bag of pee taped to his stomach are fairly obvious. *Normal*? Not so much. Awkward and constantly embarrassing? You bet.

I should pause here again and say that perhaps surprisingly, I am actually kind of grateful for that. On the most basic level, given the hand I was dealt at birth, there were no other options. I can absolutely appreciate that if my parents hadn't chosen that solution for me, I wouldn't have been able to live, period. When you only have one option, even if you don't love it, there's still room for gratitude that you have an option at all. But it probably goes without saying though that the minute any other viable alternative came along, that new possibility was going to get serious consideration.

Around my 16th birthday, my parents became aware of just such an option. A team of doctors and researchers at Indiana University had just developed a revolutionary surgical technique that created a new, "artificial" bladder, using the patient's own native intestinal tissue. The "Indiana Reservoir," as it is known, enabled patients to achieve normal bladder function via catheterization of an internal pouch. It was originally designed for patients whose previously functioning bladders had been lost to cancer or other traumas. Almost immediately, its potential was recognized for spina bifida patients as well. "Almost immediately" also accurately describes how quickly I became interested in a solution that meant the end of my then-current situation, and the beginning of a new, more *normal* life.

Sixteen-year-olds are funny, though. As I know from having been one, and as I am reminded constantly by currently living with one, they often have selective hearing – and decision making. At that age, I didn't need to hear much to be sold on what I had already embraced as a literally life-changing opportunity. I was ready to go, right then and there. Thankfully, my parents were also there listening – to ALL of the information.

If you think the process of surgically harvesting roughly three feet of small intestine, reconnecting that pathway, and then using that tissue to craft a liquid- and pressure-tight pouch, all before inserting it into a plumbing system that hadn't been used in 16 years sounds complicated – you would be right. As the doctors would explain, the surgery was MAJOR. The procedure itself would take 11-13 hours, followed by 7-10 days in the hospital, and weeks or even months of recovery thereafter.

In hindsight, I think I'm glad that 16-year-olds are often more brave than "smart." Just in revisiting the idea as I write about it now, I'm not sure that, as a man nearing 50, I would be jumping out of my seat to sign up for that. But at 16, it was a no-brainer. I knew where I was, and what I had gone through up to that point. And I knew that, God willing, there were a LOT more years ahead of me than behind. Those could be years filled with the joy of *normal* things like college, and girlfriends, and jobs and…basically all the things I couldn't even imagine experiencing in my current condition.

Welcome back to the crossroads. Yes, my parents were there to hear everything involved – and to fully understand it in ways my teenage brain surely couldn't. And yes, like countless times before, they were the adults in the room who were going to have to ultimately sign off on a minor having major surgery. But this was different. They knew it, and they wanted me to know it too. From the outset, this was going to be MY decision. It was MY life that would be impacted, and hopefully changed for the better. Only I could decide whether the risks were worth the rewards. And those

I CAN APPRECIATE THAT

stakes weren't small. On one hand, you can potentially have a life you previously thought impossible. On the other, it's a massive, reconstructive, abdominal surgery featuring a very new medical procedure that doesn't have any real historical data to demonstrate long- or even short-term success. Oh, and it's elective. Unlike those other times where if you DON'T do this, you'll likely die – this is something you're *choosing* to do, even though you also have the choice to do nothing and keep on living just like you have been. And that was the kicker. Continuing to live as I had up to that point was the one thing I didn't want; the one thing I couldn't do. My decision was made.

My parents' decision? Immediate, unwavering, unquestioned support.

I'm sure there are plenty of other (smaller and less consequential) instances of them taking the same stance before this decision. But this event sticks as a marker in my mind. It's the first of what would prove to be many times moving forward where my parents handed me an important decision and essentially said, "We love you. We trust you. We believe in you. We support you. Whatever you decide, we'll be there." I don't care if you're six, or sixteen, or sixty, there's nothing in this world more encouraging, or valuable, or genuinely appreciable, you can say to someone. In that moment, I had freedom, and power, and endorsement, and most importantly support – regardless of the outcome. Think about the decisions we make every day, big or small. How often do we get paralyzed because we don't have even ONE of those things, let alone all of them? We freeze, because we don't know what we should do, or what might happen, or what other people will think. What if that didn't happen to us, because we all had someone to stand with us? And what if it didn't happen to others because we ourselves were the ones standing next to them?

As of this writing, it's been 33 years since I made the decision to have that surgery. I can honestly say it's still one of the hardest I've ever had to make. I also don't mind admitting that I called my mom from the hospital the night before the procedure, crying and pleading for them to come get me and take me home. I was scared and didn't think I could go through with it. Her response? She listened carefully as I expressed all my fears and concerns, and then she reminded me of three things. First, she understood why I was scared and that it was perfectly reasonable. Second, she told me to remember the reasons WHY I had made the decision in the first place, and that she still believed those were valid and wise. And third, she told me flat out – "If you're not ready, or don't want to do it, we'll come get you."

Again, full trust, full endorsement, full support. I think I still probably cried myself to sleep in dread fear that night. Fear was still there, but the larger power in the room was the comfort and confidence that comes from pure, unconditional love. At the time, I didn't know that's what it was, but I've come to understand it over time. Like other things, once you know what it looks and feels like, you recognize it when it shows up again in other places. You understand the power it has in the comfort and confidence it brings, and perhaps most importantly, you realize how powerful a gift it is to give others.

I went through with the surgery. Those doctors gave me the gift of the fresh start I was looking for – the blank slate upon which I could start scripting a new life story. The first thing written on it was the lesson of empowerment and love my parents had been teaching me the whole time.

If You Could Do It All Over Again...

In the specific, short term, that surgery was a great success. But it wasn't as if at the age of 16, I discovered the magic solution to end my health challenges once and for all. Not even close. In fact, it wouldn't be until more than twice that many years later, when I was in my mid-thirties, that I would finally have had more birthdays than surgeries.

Immediately following a surgery that was supposed to change my life, shockingly, my life did NOT instantly change. Turns out, there's some baggage that takes quite a bit longer to unpack.

The Indiana Reservoir (IR) procedure was an absolute revelation, in most of the ways I'd hoped for, and even in a few I never imagined. It might sound odd, but I actually separate my life into two distinct halves – the first 16 years of my life BEFORE the IR surgery as one, and then everything AFTER it as the other. The degree to which it changed my life, and what I saw as possible as a result, is that significant.

I had been given a clean slate, but I really had no idea what to do with it. On the outside, I finally appeared a little more *normal*. But on the inside, all the garbage – the frustration and pain and self-doubt – that I had allowed to fill my head up to that point was still there. I did feel like a new person, but I had no idea who that person was, and I had to figure that out before I would ever be able to introduce him to anyone else. Of course, to my earlier point, most of the people my age that I knew – from school, church, etc. – already had a perception of me cemented in their minds. With a few exceptions, it wouldn't be until I moved to a completely new town to attend college a year and half later that I would get to really practice developing new relationships based solely on this new person I had become. And even then, it wasn't easy.

Even though any person I met from that point forward would probably only know about me what I told them, the "old" me was still there in my head, contributing its voice of doubt. Even though I felt like a new person, my physical challenges, and the way I felt about them, still impacted those new relationships. This fact was particularly true as I moved (very) slowly toward amorous ones. As the prospect of entering committed dating relationships arrived, I was petrified. On one hand, I value honesty as something which must be given and received if a relationship has any chance of lasting. Conversely, I had very little interest in sharing the embarrassing details of my medical history with anyone, let alone a girl I was trying not to repulse.

In some ways, I suppose I can also appreciate the fact that I have really only had a few very serious dating relationships. It's fewer times I've had to deliver the "if we're going to be committed to each other, there are some things about me you ought to know" talk. I've had some version of that talk exactly thrice – each time giving a little more detail than before. The last of those talks happened more than 20 years ago, with an amazing young woman named Carie, who would eventually become my wife. You'll hear a lot more about her in these stories; she's central in most of them. I can still recall us sitting together in a car, me trying very hard to work up the courage to share those still-embarrassing details and hoping her response wouldn't be the end of our relationship. Her response? Immediate, unwavering, unquestioned support. Sound familiar?

Relationship experts and psychologists will tell you that often, people seek partners who resemble their own parents when choosing a spouse. That direction can lead to mixed results, depending on your parents and their behaviors. As for me, I appreciate the picture my parents painted that showed me exactly what I should be looking for when I found Carie.

It's Not Just the Journey, It's the Company

If I'm being a little bit honest, I'll admit, I wasn't sure exactly where this particular chapter was going to take me, in terms of what I would share and what I might learn from it. If I'm being completely honest, I'd tell you that I really didn't even want to include it at all. There are plenty of things in this basket I'd rather have just sat aside – content to focus on areas and events that were perhaps equally Appreciable, but less awkward to revisit.

But as you'll see if you follow this journey a bit further, I have a pretty awesome co-pilot. As she has done countless times in our 20+ years together, my wife Carie was the one standing beside me, pushing me gently but intentionally in the direction of "difficult" things that make my life better. Down that path have been more than a few things I have discovered that are worth Appreciating. I originally suspected my medical challenges would be among the hardest places to find them, but as has been the case with this entire collection, I've been consistently and pleasantly surprised.

The more I thought about it, the more I realized that *a true understanding of relationships* themselves was probably the greatest hidden blessing waiting to be uncovered along this specific stretch of road. Certainly prior to my IR surgery – and probably for a good while after – I would say real, meaningful relationships were among what I wanted most, but thought I could never have, because I thought of myself as "unknowable."

In looking back, I see now that everything I needed was already there. Everything I would come to value and understand as part of what makes for a truly special, perhaps unbreakable, relationship was shown to me as a part of what I experienced through all of my health-related challenges. In my experience, here's the recipe:

Honesty

John 8:32 – "And you will know the truth, and the truth will set you free."

In the almost 50 years I have been walking, limping, crutching, or wheeling down this road, I've had a lot of people tell me a lot of "bad" news – or at least a lot of things I didn't appreciate. Here's one thing I definitely can Appreciate. In all that time, as it relates to my health and the challenges I was going to face, I can't think of anyone who lied to me, or even gave me false hope. Like my parents, every doctor I can remember – and there are a lot of them – gave me realistic expectations based on straight, honest facts. Sometimes they were telling me I could expect things to suck, or hurt, or take a long time. Sometimes they even told me they had no idea what to expect. But they were always honest. That honesty is

I CAN APPRECIATE THAT

a gift, because it gives you what you need to decide how to respond appropriately.

Historically, I haven't always reciprocated that gift of honesty, but these days, I'm trying my best to do exactly that. I'm trying to stop hiding things from people out of fear they won't understand and start trusting that maybe they will. Or at least stop caring if they don't.

Loyalty

Proverbs 27:10 – "Do not forsake your friend and your father's friend... better is a neighbor who is near than a brother who is far away."

Proverbs 17:17 – "A friend loves at all times, and a brother is born for adversity."

When for most of your early life, real friends seem hard to come by, you develop a certain appreciation for the few you do have – and a real resistance to letting them go. I learned some hard lessons early on about the difference between people who would stick with me – when it wasn't easy for *them*, let alone me – and those who wouldn't or couldn't. A lot of that is the insecurity and ignorance of youth, which is very forgivable, but the lesson still sticks.

Once you give me a reason to care about you – and unless you then go out of your way to give me a reason NOT to – if I'm with you, I'm WITH you. For better or worse, I can be hard to shake. Ask a few of those folks who stuck by me from way back in the "bad old days." I'm still here, and I'm not leaving.

Trust

Proverbs 3:5 – "Trust in the Lord with all your heart, and do not lean on your own understanding."

I don't know everything. In fact, I know next to nothing. The only way we make it in this world is by understanding that we can't do everything by ourselves – and we shouldn't WANT to.

Sometimes you have to rely on other people – and that means trusting that they won't hurt you. Sometimes we get burned by that, but most of the time, trusting someone is the down payment on an investment that beautifully and profoundly appreciates in value.

Before my IR surgery, we asked doctors if this was a lifelong solution, or more of a stop-gap fix. Before I committed, I wanted to know, "how long will this work?" Again, with honesty, they said, "We don't know. It hasn't been around long enough to study that." Without trust in their ability, I couldn't have gone through with it, and I would have missed every other blessing that has come as a result.

It's probably easier to trust people like surgeons, experts in things we ourselves know nothing about, as opposed to all the other *average* people we encounter every day. But maybe it shouldn't be. It's hard and scary to think about opening yourself up to that, but more often than not, it's worth it.

Respect

Philippians 2:3 – "Do nothing from rivalry or conceit, but in humility count others more significant than yourselves."

Matthew 7:12 - "So whatever you wish that others would do to you, do also to them, for this is the Law and the Prophets."

And speaking of trusting those around us more universally, here's one thing you can absolutely count on. Every person you encounter is dealing with challenges you know nothing about. This reality demands we approach each other with kindness, grace, and respect.

This is a bit of a double-edged sword. In my case, what I really wanted for so long was for people to give me the benefit of the doubt – to see me as *normal*, even if I clearly was different – and to respect that even though I may have certain deficiencies, I also had talents that were far more worthy of their focus.

Turns out, now, as I approach 50, I actually don't mind a little extra consideration for those challenges. Thirty or forty years ago, I would get angry when people would point out my differences. Now, when I park my car in certain spaces, people sometimes actually ask me, "Are you even really handicapped?" – presumably because their assumption is that only people in wheelchairs need or deserve those spaces. Those moments make me angry, too, but what they're really saying, in different words is "You shouldn't be there; you look *normal*". So, basically, I'm getting mad when people give me what I've wanted all along? Sometimes, it's hard to remember which part of that paradox I should appreciate more.

Empathy

1 Corinthians 12:26 – "If one member suffers, all suffer together; if one member is honored, all rejoice together."

Colossians 3:12 – "Put on then, as God's chosen ones, holy and beloved, compassionate hearts, kindness, humility, meekness, and patience."

And finally, and perhaps most importantly, there is empathy. The ability to understand how another person feels about something we ourselves are not experiencing is among the greatest gifts we can give or receive. It's also highly attractive in relationships and valuable beyond measure in friendships. We've all been in places where someone else can't actually solve our problem for us. But just knowing that another human understands and cares about the difficulty we're facing makes a huge difference in our ability to survive, and ultimately thrive.

I spent too many years believing that while a few people might have cared, nobody actually *understood* my situation. That thought made my heart harder and my mind more cynical than they should ever be.

Discovering that, in some cases, understanding had always been there, and that it would grow over time as I and the people around me got further in our journeys of life, has made my heart soft again. And best of all, it prepared me to fully Appreciate the gift of empathy by sharing it with others.

As you'll see in some of the stories that follow here, my world is full of children. In my various roles as a parent, coach, school and church volunteer, and occasional foster parent, I interact with kids constantly. The world they are growing up in today is vastly different than the one of my childhood. But I know for sure they're all struggling with something they think nobody else gets. I've been there. I know how that feels, and I know the difference it makes when somebody feeds the basic human need to be seen and understood. If the single benefit of walking this road is the opportunity to encourage those who are just starting their own journey and can't yet see all the blessings hidden in the obstacles that lie ahead, that might be enough all on its own.

Honesty. Loyalty. Trust. Respect. Empathy. When I look at the best, most solid, most rewarding relationships in my life, this is the recipe. Yours might be different, and that's perfectly fine. These are the blocks I use, because they're the ones other people have used to help build the person I am today.

This is Heavy; I'm Putting it Down Now

You might have noticed that throughout this section I have placed the word *"normal"* in italics nearly every time it appears. That's because it's the concept I was most fixated on, and frankly most worried about, in sharing this part of my story.

The primary benefit of this exercise is all the things I've come to realize and understand through the process of writing these stories. So, here comes the (probably not-) shocking revelation of this chapter:

I'm not normal. And guess what? Neither are you – because no one is, and that's more than okay.

In Psalm 139:14, David celebrates God, telling Him: *"I praise you because I am fearfully and wonderfully made; your works are wonderful, I know that full well."*

I'm here to claim the same Truth.

For better or worse, by writing this book and including this chapter, I'm essentially telling the entire world most of what I think is "wrong" or abnormal about me. That's okay too.

All that stuff I tried very hard for decades to hide, ignore, and wish away; I'm just gonna put it out there. I'm tired of carrying all that garbage I've had strapped to my back for most of my life. I'm ready to unpack it, set it down, and finally move forward without its weight. That's a gift I honestly never anticipated receiving when my son's question initially sparked me to sit, think, and write. Man, I can Appreciate that.

Questions to Consider:

• How "normal" has your life been? Is that a good or bad thing?

• What's the biggest decision of your life that involved you having to trust someone else? For better or worse, what can you appreciate about how that turned out?

• As you walk through life, who are the people who have been, and still are, always there for you? Have you told them how much you appreciate that?

• What burdens are you carrying right now that are long overdue to be put down? What's stopping you?

Wisdom to Appreciate:

John 8:32 – "And you will know the truth, and the truth will set you free."

Proverbs 3:5 – "Trust in the Lord with all your heart, and do not lean on your own understanding."

Matthew 7:12 - "So whatever you wish that others would do to you, do also to them, for this is the Law and the Prophets."

1 Corinthians 12:26 – "If one member suffers, all suffer together; if one member is honored, all rejoice together."

Psalm 139:14 - "I praise you because I am fearfully and wonderfully made; your works are wonderful, I know that full well."

Chapter 3:
My Greatest Enemy, and Opportunity

This next tale is a bit long because, like life itself, it's really several stories woven into one connected narrative. And, fair warning, it's a bit of a roller coaster. There are high points and some very low lows, but if you want to know how the single worst thing that ever happened to me ultimately taught me how to grieve, how to love, how to trust, and how to honor others – come with me; it's probably worth the ride.

If There's One Thing I Hate...

For many years now, I have made a real effort to honestly say that there is no one or nothing that I genuinely hate. And for even longer, as I held tightly to negative feelings about one thing or another, I've known that hatred is a giant waste of time and energy. It's genuinely the most unproductive emotion we experience. And yet, there was one *thing* I still allowed myself to hate. For decades, I reserved a little black pit in my soul in which I let the darkest, most sincere hatred fester for one particular entity – cancer.

As I think about it now, over the past couple of decades, I have dedicated a staggering amount of time and energy to hating cancer. In fact, as this project began to form in my head, and I started to think through what it would likely cover, I had a terrible realization. Whether I liked it or not, one of these chapters was going to be about cancer.

Why? Well, if the point of this entire exercise is revisiting challenging times in my life, and viewing them through a different lens, then cancer is probably the Mount Everest of those treks. By that, I mean, it's by far the biggest hill for me to climb. In fact, the specter of cancer feels like a dark cloud that has hovered over most of my life at this point. It's definitely not something I can say I've "gotten over" either. I don't mind admitting I was extremely doubtful I would find ANYTHING I could say I "appreciated" about cancer at the beginning of this process. But you know what they say about the healing power of time, too, right?

Speaking of time, let's start at the beginning.

Not My Best Friend!

Until I was 19 years old, I don't think I knew or was even aware of anyone who had cancer. And then, as anyone touched by this horrible disease can attest, in the blink of an eye, everything changes.

In 1992, I was a sophomore at the University of South Carolina. My sister, two years older, was a senior at Auburn University. Although we fought like any other siblings, we were close growing up. While I was the "weird" kid who, because of constant medical issues and surgeries, often got teased or bullied by other kids for being "different," Kim was golden-girl popular. Pretty, smart, athletic, talented, etc. – she was all of that. She was somehow able to be friends with everyone, including me. And, for someone like me, who struggled to find a lot of real friendships in childhood, that was a big deal. Our relationship looked different at various ages, but the bottom line for me was that from about the age of 8 or 9, whether she felt the same or not, my sister was basically my best friend.

We went through school together, her always two years ahead, blazing a trail in front of me and showing me places to tread and others to avoid. She introduced me to movies, books, and music the way older siblings often do for their younger ones. She gave me a barometer and a compass, always for what was "cool" and usually what was "right." She even begrudgingly made space for me in her social life, tolerating me existing in the same space with her and her cooler, older friends after football games and at parties. So, when she left for college at the start of my junior year of high school, I got a taste of what it would be like to miss her. Suddenly, I was on my own at home and socially. By then, I had a small group of close friends, but it was still a significant loss to have a constant companion suddenly gone.

We would see each other when she came home on breaks, or the few times I went to visit her at Auburn. Those couple of years were truly transitional. She became more of an adult every time I saw her - living independently, joining a sorority, and meeting the man who would become her husband one day. By the time I went to school at Carolina two years later, our relationship had evolved. There's a permanence to siblinghood that transcends physical distance or even time. As siblings growing up, you know a great many things will change. You know each of you will get older, move to new places, get jobs, find relationships, maybe have kids, etc. But you also assume some things, like your basic dynamic with each other, will always be the same.

But, near the end of 1991, everything started to change. I wasn't even aware at the time, but Kim had gone to the doctor. She was concerned about a mole that had formed on her breast. Today, given medical advancements, a young woman making the same discovery who proactively seeks care would have pretty good chances of an ultimately positive outcome, even with a troubling initial diagnosis. Unfortunately, Kim's story plays out very differently. For starters, Kim was not proactive. Paralyzed by fear and lack of information, she waited.

She waited to tell our parents. And after she did tell our mom about the discovery of the mole, she waited a crucial couple of months, neglecting mom's initial advice to see a dermatologist. She waited until it wasn't just a possibility, but rather a certainty that something was wrong, before asking for help. When she finally did take action, my parents called a doctor in Atlanta, and she had an appointment the next day where the mole was removed and sent for testing. A few days later, results revealed they needed to take more, ultimately about a quarter of her breast. The dermatologist suggested all the compromised tissue was removed, and only bi-annual check-ups were required for maintenance. Taking that doctor at his word, Kim and the rest of us took a deep breath and went on with life.

Six months later, in June of 1992, Kim graduated from Auburn University. By that time, she was already seriously dating a young man named Dennis, whom she had met at school. For graduation, my parents took her on a celebratory trip to Hawaii, an event that would end up teaching me one of the hardest lessons I've ever had to learn. My parents intended for all four of us to go. I had recently had surgery and was unsure how well I could walk and how much time I could spend in the water. That, coupled with a budding relationship of my own, led me to decline a FREE trip to Hawaii. Yeah, you read that right. Even if this story weren't about what it's about, I would still want to go back in time in punch 20-year-old me in the face for being so stupid and selfish. In what is probably the single most glaring incidence of lack of appreciation in my whole life, I decided to stay home by myself in Atlanta while my parents and sister went to Hawaii. As only an immature quasi-adult could, I completely missed the once-in-lifetime nature of that opportunity. Thirty years later, I realize how unlikely it is that anyone else is ever going to offer me a free trip to Hawaii. But that's not the worst of it, not by a longshot. What I also decided, in ignorance, was that I had plenty of TIME for things like that. *"We've got our whole lives ahead of us; this is something I can do later, when and if I want."* It's a decision I regret to this day and probably will for as long as I live.

A few short weeks after they returned from that trip, Kim developed a lump under her arm that swelled quickly and hurt. Having learned not to wait from her previous experience, she immediately went to an oncologist for an exam. They surgically removed the lump and some surrounding lymph nodes and sent the tissues for biopsy. In July of 1992, we would learn that Kim, at the age of 22, and seemingly a picture of youth, beauty, and near-perfect health, was diagnosed with malignant melanoma – an aggressive form of skin cancer.

The picture I've painted so far is dark, and it gets darker. But it's also incomplete without the surprising points of light that exist in the same canvas. While I was in South Carolina, trying my best at my parents' insistence to keep moving on my own path, my sister was doing a remarkable job of living her best life. In the face of unprecedented challenges, she was working hard to Appreciate the opportunities that lay before her.

Almost immediately upon her diagnosis, Kim began chemotherapy, and within weeks, radiation therapy. Those treatments quickly took a toll on her physically. But her spirit stayed strong, in large part, I think, because of the positive possibilities in front of her. In August, just a month or so after her diagnosis, Kim had one of the most memorable and powerful experiences of her life.

Dennis, Kim's boyfriend of two years at that point, took her to Stone Mountain Park near our home in suburban Atlanta. There, from the top of that mountain, with the whole world at their feet, he asked for her hand in marriage. She accepted, of course, and we were all thrilled.

Under normal circumstances, an engagement is cause for great celebration. In this case, it was true ten-fold. I think it's safe to say that high on any parent's list of hopes is for their children to be happy. As far as relationships go, parents can only hope their children choose wisely and end up with partners who love, honor, care for, respect, cherish and appreciate them. In every aspect, Kim could not have chosen a better mate. While no one is perfect, Dennis was undoubtedly the perfect gift from God to her, and us, in this time.

Here they were, in their early twenties, newly graduated from college, seemingly with their entire lives ahead of them. And then the train comes off the tracks. Of course, their relationship began, developed, and solidified outside of the shadow of cancer. And though not yet engaged, they were already fully committed to one another by the time of Kim's diagnosis. But that doesn't mean Dennis didn't have choices. Learning of her diagnosis, and later her prognosis, and seeing the likely challenges ahead, Dennis could have decided that it was "too much," or somehow "not worth it" to hold onto their love in the face of such adversity. He could have just walked away, but he didn't. He stayed and fought alongside her every step of the way, and in the process, Dennis gave me a gift I don't think I recognized, understood, or fully appreciated until years later.

At this point, I was 20 years old with little relationship experience myself. Like all of us, I had the example of my parents to follow. For some, that may be less than ideal, but I was exceptionally fortunate. From near bankruptcy to familial medical issues, my parents have had at least their fair share of marriage-testing struggles, if not more. And while those episodes weren't fun or pretty, they managed to come through all of it very much intact. As of this writing, my parents have recently celebrated their 50th wedding anniversary. Along with Carie's parents (who also reached their Silver milestone in the same year), they continue to be stellar examples of what a marriage should be.

All of that is great. But, until you reach a particular season of life, your appreciation for marriage can be pretty limited in terms of both its value and its difficulty. As a child, you might not even think about it. As a teenager, you start to become aware of relationships, and your parents become models for that. In young adulthood, your sphere of influencers expands to include people your own age. You start looking at your siblings, cousins, or friends for images of healthy relationships. So, back to Dennis, as there's an important distinction there I've only recently realized.

This Is What Love Looks Like

The view we have of our parents' marriages is often tinted. We may see the current state, but the context for how they got there is incomplete. We didn't see them grow up together or watch them learn HOW to have their current relationship. We may see them living out the wedding vows they made decades ago, but not necessarily what came before. In Dennis and Kim's relationship, even though most of it was happening hundreds of miles away, I was still getting to *see* how that developed – first as a friendship, then as something more, and finally, as a commitment born of mutual respect and genuine love

In some cases, it seems like people view marriage as a finite moment in time, with different realities on either side of that specific moment. For some, it's as if there's an invisible commitment clock that doesn't really start running until they say "I do." Think about it. Bachelor and bachelorette parties often include shenanigans that are casually explained away or discounted by the mentality of *"it doesn't count; we're not married yet."* So, here's the distinction. In Dennis' case, he knew with painful clarity the situation to which he was committing. Long before they stood at the altar and pledged themselves to each other "in sickness and in health," they were already living their vows. There were eight months between their engagement and Kim and Dennis' wedding; eight months full of declining health and increasing stress. And yet, what I realize now is that while their wedding happened on February 23rd, 1993, that day itself was almost purely ceremonial. They had already been *married*, in spirit and practice, for more than a year by then.

As you can imagine, or might even know from experience, watching a loved one battle and ultimately succumb to an illness like cancer is heartbreaking. You can also likely imagine the heart-filling encouragement that comes from seeing other people care for your loved one as much, or in their way, even more than you do. For that alone, Dennis will always have a special place in my and my parents' hearts and lives. That's *forever* stuff, and among

I CAN APPRECIATE THAT

the many reasons we will always consider him and his family part of ours. But the real gift Dennis gave me was even more valuable – because it's a gift I have been able to Appreciate in my own marriage. In demonstrating his love for my sister, Dennis showed me – with even greater clarity than my parents could at the time – what being a spouse truly means. It looks a lot like the directives we see in 1 Corinthians 13:4-8, which is precisely why this particular passage gets recited at so many weddings:

"4 Love is patient, love is kind. It does not envy, it does not boast, it is not proud. 5 It does not dishonor others, it is not self-seeking, it is not easily angered, it keeps no record of wrongs. 6 Love does not delight in evil but rejoices with the truth. 7 It always protects, always trusts, always hopes, always perseveres. 8 Love never fails."

Those are pretty words and a noble standard when pledging yourself to another person "until death do you part." It's something else to see those words get LIVED out. And altogether different when a man is pledging them to your sister/best friend, especially when the worst-case scenario is anything but hypothetical. Suddenly, those words take on new levels of meaning and seriousness. I know they have for me.

When you see firsthand what unwavering commitment looks like, and you can understand the value it has – it's incredibly easy to be grateful for that example. And that, in turn, empowers you to fully Appreciate the lesson – growing its value by applying it in your own life. I know for sure my marriage with Carie is influenced by the example Dennis gave me for how to handle challenges – even existential ones – with grace, strength, and resolve. Like all couples, Carie and I have had our struggles. And I'm thankful beyond words our marriage thus far hasn't been tested anywhere near the degree to which Dennis and Kim's was. But even though it came at a cost I'd never want to pay, I'm most grateful for the unique appreciation I gained for the concept of commitment in general. My parents, and Carie's, set the bar high for what a solid marriage looks like, and Dennis came along and raised it even higher. It's a standard I continuously strive to maintain for myself and increasingly to model for our boys as they start to look at us for cues in their relationships.

In Sickness and In Health

Kim's relationship with Dennis is one of the silver linings of the larger story of her journey with cancer. And the lesson it taught me is one of the best and most positive, but it's only one of the things I've learned to Appreciate through her struggle.

Let's jump back a little bit. Those eight months between Dennis and Kim's engagement and their wedding were eventful. Though undergoing chemo and other treatments, Kim remained hopeful and focused on planning their wedding. She and Dennis traveled to Ohio to visit some of our family and attend a shower in their honor, even though she was sick and tired most of the time.

In early January 1993, we awoke and greeted the day like it was any other, but it wasn't. When Kim didn't come downstairs as usual, my mom went to check on her and found Kim incoherent and unable to move. She called 911, and an ambulance came to take Kim to the hospital. It was there we would learn that cancer spread to her brain, causing a stroke. Further tests revealed more spread into her bones and an inoperable tumor in her chest. To relieve her pain, they severed a nerve in her neck, which helped but resulted in her losing the use of her right arm.

My recollection of the fine details here is fuzzy for a couple of reasons. Primarily, these events occurred over twenty years ago now. As I thought back in preparation for writing this, my memory created an incomplete picture. Here again, I'm grateful to my parents for graciously revisiting these events with me to help fill in the gaps.

Aside from the time-lapse, there are other reasons for my lack of clarity. First, I was a sophomore in college, living 200 miles from home. My parents were adamant that even though Kim was sick, I should remain in school. And even though I don't know exactly what I could have done to help, I don't think I appreciated that decision at the time either. In hindsight, I recognize that, as they had done on several occasions regarding my health, my parents were trying to choose from a list of terrible options, and they were simply doing what they thought was best for everyone. I'm sure they were right. Until you're in that situation yourself, it's probably impossible to appreciate just how gut-wrenching those decisions must be. I pray I never experience the other side of that scenario myself.

Staying in school did insulate me from directly confronting this situation, but it also isolated me. Away from family and surrounded by friends, I could hide from some of the immediate pain I would have experienced at home, but I also chose some pretty unhealthy places to hide. I drank a lot, or at least a lot for me, and became a habitual user of marijuana. I probably would have engaged in some of those behaviors anyway but blurring a reality I didn't want to face gave me an all-too-convenient "excuse" to do so, and in excess.

But even though there are aspects of Kim's journey that I struggled to recall, there are others that remain crystal clear. Some of those are wonderful; others most definitely are not. Among the positive highlights, of course, was their wedding. Despite all the challenges they faced and setting aside their fears of what lay ahead, on February 23rd, 1993, Dennis and Kim were married at our family's church in Atlanta. She was in considerable pain, noticeably weak, and nowhere near strong enough to enjoy the day as she deserved to, but it was joyous nonetheless. Hundreds of family members and friends joined us for the celebration. Most of the attendees were well aware of her situation and status. And yet, there was joy and a celebration of a love that had already bloomed in full.

I had a wonderful time at their wedding and will carry fond memories of that day with me forever. Those memories aside, it's what I've realized in hindsight that I'll try most to Appreciate. I don't know how many weddings I've been to since 1993 – it's a lot. But at some point, I know I started viewing them a little differently. Now, whenever I attend a wedding, I find myself praying for the couple. I pray both the bride and groom share Dennis' understanding of what it means to be a spouse. I pray they are already married in spirit before they approach the altar and not hoping that the physical act of reciting vows or exchanging rings will create a dynamic between them that doesn't already exist. I pray they have a community of family and friends who will support them and even fight with them to protect their marriage. And I pray they don't disregard the Hand of Time, thinking they have an abundance of that most precious resource, when the truth is, none of us will ever know how much of it we have. I feel confident if all that is true, those marriages not only start from a place of strength but are also well positioned to appreciate in value over time.

The Truth Hurts

I also took lessons from Kim's experience that were much less joyous but appreciable all the same. One of these came courtesy of an interaction I had with one of the doctors who attended Kim near the end of her care. We were in the hospital during the testing that revealed Kim's cancer had spread significantly. My parents had already spoken with this doctor and were probably talking with another. For whatever reason, I found myself alone with that doctor and away from my parents. I had only heard a portion of his report, but I recall him saying that the cancer had spread to her brain. I don't know why, perhaps shock or a lack of filters that comes from fear, anger, and immaturity, but at that moment, I asked him probably the most direct question I could have.

"Is my sister going to die?"

That doctor looked directly at me and, without a moment's hesitation, replied, matter-of-factly, "Yes. I'm very sorry."

His response was shocking. And if you're guessing that I didn't exactly appreciate it in real-time, you'd be right. I'd asked the question in a moment of panic, so it wasn't a calculated exchange where I was counting on a specific answer. I'm sure subconsciously, I probably expected him to offer some comfort or hope. Instead, as painful as it was, he gave me something else – the truth. And that was the end of our conversation: one question and one answer. Still in shock, I walked out of the front door of the hospital alone and broke down.

I think about that exchange often. I had never met that doctor before, so I don't know if his reply to me was consistent with his overall bedside manner or not. I don't know what else he had going on or what he thought when I asked him. For years, I wondered why he didn't lie to me or at least say something like, "we're doing everything we can," or "let's wait and see," or even "we just don't know." For years, I was sure I would have appreciated ambiguity much more than honesty in that situation. Decades later, I've found a way to Appreciate that experience too.

In my line of work as an advertising writer, I don't ever encounter situations with life-and-death consequences. The results of even my worst professional decisions might be that I, or someone else, could lose some money or a job. That's about it. And it's improbable anyone is ever going to ask me the question I asked that doctor. But I can still learn from the way he answered it.

In my original estimation, his answer's brute force was unkind and might have even felt like a form of disrespect. How could he be so blunt or care so little for my feelings? In hindsight, it's easier to see that honesty – even excruciating honesty – is far more respectful and useful than the alternatives. When you have the truth, you can at least do your best to make a plan to react in the most productive and appropriate way to whatever situation you're facing.

Whether it be my wife, my children, my friends, my colleagues, or even someone I've never met, I owe everyone that level of honesty – we all do. That's not to say we should go around making a point of telling everyone every painful truth. That would probably be unkind in a completely different way. But when the rubber meets the road, in those times when we face difficult questions, and we know the answers might be uncomfortable, we owe it to others and ourselves to have the same courage of conviction that doctor had in telling me the truth.

By telling me the truth, I don't think that doctor made the situation any easier. It probably made it much harder. I don't know if I've ever even talked to my parents about that exchange either, but I know it impacted how I moved forward and how I processed and ultimately dealt with what would eventually happen.

After Dennis and Kim's wedding, they went for a quick honeymoon trip to the beach in Destin, Florida. She tried her best to enjoy the experience and relax, but when they returned after a few days, she was in so much pain the doctors decided to put her on a morphine drip IV to offer relief. Quickly thereafter, she lost her appetite and started getting confused, including about where she was and who we were.

On April 13th, 1993, only a month after their brief honeymoon at the beach, Kim went back to the hospital with more complications. The doctors told my parents nothing else could be done for her, and they arranged to take Kim home with a hospice nurse.

Again, at the behest of my parents, who were trying to make the best decisions possible, I had returned to school in South Carolina. When they called to update me on the situation, I was not doing well. Shaken by the scenario in general and the doctor's stark admission, I had turned to both prayer and self-medication for solace. In those months near the end, I prayed hard – harder than I ever had for myself in any of my own challenges, or anyone else, for that matter. I also probably drank harder and made other poor choices to try and numb myself out of thinking about it.

My parents called and told me I needed to come home, which I did immediately. They had taken Kim home and told a few close friends to come to visit. I drove the 200 miles from Columbia to

Atlanta in record time that day, almost daring the police to pull me over for speeding. I arrived to find Kim in a hospital bed, unresponsive and resting. I asked my parents for a few minutes alone with her, which, of course they granted. I had never had to say goodbye to anyone like that before, let alone my sister. I spent a quiet moment reeling, feeling utterly helpless, and having no idea what to do. Through tears, I thanked her for being my first best friend and always protecting, supporting, and loving me. I asked her to watch over me, knowing I was in troubled times and likely headed for more. I held her hand, said more prayers, and kissed her forehead, hoping she could hear me, even if she couldn't speak. With a final "I love you," I relinquished the room and went outside. A short while later, with Dennis and my mom by her side, my sister Kim passed away.

With her passing came everything you would expect: profound sadness, shock, despair, and anger – so much anger. I was mad at everyone and everything. Mad at cancer for taking her, and worst of all, mad as hell at God for ignoring or denying my many prayers. That was April of 1993, the end of my sister's life on Earth and the beginning of my crisis of faith that would persist for decades. There *is* actually something to Appreciate in that as well, but it took me a LONG time and a few more episodes in this chapter to find it. The next lesson in this journey came from somewhere else entirely.

Kim passed away at age 23. I had just turned 21 a few weeks earlier. Like most people that age, I had been to very few funerals up to that point. Besides two of my grandparents, I had never known anyone else who had died, and certainly no one my age. As was the case with so much of this episode, my parents did a remarkable job protecting me from the details. I can't even imagine, and thus still can't fully appreciate the levels of pure sadness and grief that must come from having to make funeral arrangements for your child. And yet, both of my parents soldiered on, managing to keep themselves, their marriage, the business they owned, and their remaining child (who was now a young adult bending toward apathy, anger, and self-destruction) afloat. I didn't see much of the planning of Kim's funeral, but I can only imagine it must have been awful. The event itself, though still one of the saddest days of my life, turned out to hold a couple of crucial lessons for me though.

A Prescription for Healing

For starters, and the thought of this being comparative makes me bristle, as it's not my intent, but... a few decades later, I've unfortunately attended several funerals, so I now have some points of reference. For example, the funeral of a high school friend of mine (a police officer killed in a traffic accident) rightly drew hundreds of family, friends, and colleagues. Besides his, I've never seen so many people gathered in one place to honor someone's life as I did at Kim's service.

That day was a bit of a blur. There was still a sense of disbelief that it was even happening. And having never really been in that situation, I had no idea what I was supposed to do or say. I do remember one particular feeling, though, a terrible feeling that lingered for years afterward. I sat there at the funeral service, and even though I was surrounded by hundreds of people who had come to support my parents and me, I couldn't help but feel utterly and profoundly ALONE. Again, the comparative nature of this thought is embarrassing, but it was genuinely true. Amongst the hundreds gathered there, NO ONE had lost what I did when Kim died, and NO ONE could understand what I felt. Awfully and selfishly, I thought that because my parents had each other – each capable of understanding the other's pain in losing a child – that perhaps that load was made somehow lighter. That's ludicrous. And Dennis, his pain of losing a wife and chosen best friend was uniquely terrible too, but in my mind at the time, I let myself believe that because he had only known Kim for a few short years by then, somehow that grief was also different to what I felt. Many people there that day would probably rightfully call Kim their best friend, but I couldn't see that either. In my head, I was the only person there, or on the entire planet, who was Kim's sibling. I was the only person there for whom she was my best friend for literally my whole life. These selfish comparisons are among the worst thoughts I've ever held, and I'm embarrassed still today to even admit to them. But I share them for an important reason. They illustrate the degree to which I felt utterly alone in the darkest time of my life. I built myself a terrible little hole to hide in and wrapped myself in a blanket of despair, convincing myself that nobody could understand, or appreciate, precisely what I was going through. And worst of all, I'd turned my back on God, too, assuming he'd just done the same to me. That's a terrible place to be, and one which you can only understand if you've been there yourself. I don't wish that on anyone, but stick with me, and I'll tell you why I can now Appreciate that experience too.

At that funeral service, I'm sure I spoke to a lot of people. And most of those conversations were brief and remarkably similar. Many of the attendees were my parents' age, or Kim's friends apart from me, so aside from them sharing their condolences, there wasn't much to say. Most of them simply said they were sorry for our loss. Some added that they were praying for us. In a complete emotional fog, a lot of that blurs together to the point where not much truly sticks out. But one thing did.

Somewhere in that foggy procession, I ended up talking with some older friends. They were my parents' age, but also the parents of one of my closest friends, and I had come to think of them as parental figures as well. I'm sure I'm paraphrasing here, but that's okay because the lasting memory of their sentiment is what really matters. What they told me was this: "I'm so sorry this happened. There's nothing I can say that will make you feel better right now. I honestly don't know how best to help you. What I DO know is that I love you, and no matter what you need me for, I'm here for you."

Okay, maybe read that again. In those four simple statements is everything: sympathy for one's loss; admission of grief and permission to feel it; acceptance of momentary helplessness; an expression of genuine love; a blank check to cash against future emotional needs; and perhaps most powerfully, kinship. There, in those few precious sentences, are the recipe for surviving grief. That's the best part. The worst part? I don't think I even heard those words consciously in real time. I spent years hurting outside of the wisdom and comfort they offer. And it would be many more years before I would rediscover them, but thankfully, they stuck somewhere in my subconscious because I would need them again one day.

I don't mean to suggest that the words of all those many other well-wishers were somehow lost on me or unimportant. They weren't. I can't tell you how affirming and encouraging it is to be among hundreds of people gathered to honor the life of someone you hold dear – that's truly awe-inspiring. It is incredible, though, how one simple conversation can hold the kernel of hope and truth that has the potential to help you, and others, appreciate a situation as awful as the death of a loved one.

What I was feeling then, that feeling I embraced for so long, was that I was ALONE. Alone in my experience and alone in the pain it brought me. What my friend was telling me was that I absolutely was NOT. They were right. All that mattered from there was what I chose to believe.

My sister passed away on April 15th, 1993. For almost 20 years, cancer would be an enemy I would loathe, and hate, and sometimes fight, from a distance. By that, I mean only that it would seemingly keep its claws off of people I knew personally for a few years. That was fine with me. Even without that personal effect, I was still taking the loss of Kim plenty personally – in some ways, I still do, and probably always will.

My parents, in their typically remarkable way, threw themselves into the battle. My mom took a break from co-piloting the business she and my dad owned together and decided to pursue a different career – in nursing. Quite a veer, but completely understandable. She has always been a caretaker, and following Kim's death, that desire magnified intensely. Ultimately, it wasn't the path for her, but it was a response that made perfect sense in the moment. They also became heavily involved with the American Cancer Society. Starting as simple volunteers, they would go on to leadership roles within their county chapter, directing and implementing its annual Relay for Life event in their local community, as well as other initiatives. In the decades since we lost Kim, they've helped raise hundreds of thousands of dollars and immeasurable quantities of awareness for cancer research in her name. Pouring your time, energy, and talent into doing whatever you can to help keep other people from sharing your experience is an inspiring response to grief and an awesome way to Appreciate that experience. It's also just part of the fantastic example they continue to set for me in so many facets of life – an example I'm still trying to Appreciate myself.

So, that's the beginning of the story of my relationship with the demon that is cancer. It's not the end, though, nor is it the end of the lessons that journey wants to keep teaching me. For those, I'm going to need to introduce you to a few other people.

Several years after Kim's death, the enemy of cancer would give me yet another opportunity to learn and grow. In the fall of 2014, my sons were seven and nine years old. As they had for many seasons before, they played baseball in our local recreational league. They were among hundreds of kids, playing a game they loved, with carefree joy and very few worries – just as it should be for children. We had played in this same league for years, and through them playing and me coaching many of their teams, we grew to know a lot of the families there. Every season, that sphere would increase, as each team would inevitably include kids we already knew, plus some new additions. To a lesser degree, we also met or at least saw kids and families from other teams during games. And even though you might not spend a ton of time with most of those kids or families, relationships certainly develop.

Like so many other endeavors, recreational baseball is a social activity with a high degree of community. The coaches are the players' parents, and with a few exceptions, many of them coach for several years consecutively. So, you're around the same people regularly and develop relationships there too. During practices and before or after games, you routinely chat with the other coaches, sharing stories of your teams' ups and downs. Through this water-cooler-talk, you end up hearing and learning little bits about lots of kids and families.

It was in this limited capacity that I first became aware of a young boy named Lake Bozman. Lake was a few months older than my youngest son and played in the same league, but not on the same team. In talking with another coach, he told me that his team included a boy who had cancer. We had played games against their team previously, and I had not noticed any players with obvious physical limitations. From the distance of my untrained, unaware eyes, Lake blended in with the rest of the players and appeared to be just another young boy among many on a field playing with his friends. I had no idea that he had already been fighting cancer for almost half of his young life by this point. And it wouldn't be until years later that I would come to know most of the details of his remarkable story and would gain a much fuller appreciation for the impact it has had and continues to have for so many.

Lake Bozman was diagnosed with AML (acute myeloid leukemia) in May 2012 at the age of five. Upon diagnosis, he went through four separate rounds of intense chemotherapy. He responded well and went into remission that October. Unfortunately, cancer returned just a few months later, in April of 2013. Lake again underwent chemotherapy and full-body radiation in preparation for a bone marrow transplant, which he received in August. Again, he responded positively. With 100% donor cells, Lake was doing well. That stabilization lasted just short of a year.

In May of 2014, one day before his 8th birthday, Lake relapsed. Worse, the doctors determined his case was unlikely to remiss again in response to further treatment. He was labeled "terminal."

Now, recall this is where I entered the story. That other coach had told me about his player with cancer, and as I said before, I wouldn't have noticed anything out of the ordinary without him mentioning it. But by the time he shared this with me, Lake had already been through more than most people could even imagine. And to the average person, those unaware or not paying attention, there was no real outward evidence of his struggle at all.

There's an often-quoted thought, which depending on the source, has a few variations. As attributed to author Wendy Mass, it says, "Be kind. Everyone you meet is fighting a battle you know nothing about." For me, this sentiment is now forever linked with Lake. And at this point, I still hadn't even *met* him. Eventually, I would, and I wish with all my heart that my story of Lake was mostly about all the great memories I have of actually spending time with him. I do have a couple of those memories, but instead, my story of Lake is that of a nine-year-old boy who is simultaneously someone I only spent a handful of minutes with and one of the most influential people I will ever know.

As fall gave way to winter, Lake would continue to receive chemotherapy to keep his cancer at bay for as long as possible. Baseball was in a long break between seasons, so I wouldn't see him for a while. At that point, I had met his family, but it's not as if we were close – I was just a random guy who coached a different team in the same league where they played baseball. I was aware of him and his situation, but in part because he seemed to be doing well with his treatments, and also because from my distant view, the worst-case scenario didn't even seem possible to me, Lake wasn't really on my radar during the end of 2014.

A few months later, coaches gathered for the beginning of the Spring 2015 season. Like most other rec leagues, we watched kids try out, evaluated them, and then did our best to draft teams with a competitive balance in terms of the players' skills. As we discussed players, it came up that Lake's name was among those on the registration. The same coach who had Lake on his team the previous fall spoke up. He mentioned that Lake was sick, and he wasn't sure if he could even play. He added that he had developed a relationship with the family and would like to continue being his coach. We all agreed without further conversation. In hindsight, though, it's a great example of what we loved so much about this particular baseball league. We all had special relationships with certain players and families, some to the extent that they even became like family. But it didn't occur to me until later that Lake was in the perfect hands there, too. Of course, Lake should be with a coach whose heart already understood his situation and the unique circumstances it would require – a heart born from building that special relationship none of the rest of us had. Something like that can go completely unnoticed when a group of middle-aged men are competing to build winning squads of 8-year-old baseball players. In the end, that level of relationship makes a huge difference.

That spring season started like any other. As we practiced and prepared to play, we'd see the same kids and families come and go, saying 'hi' casually in passing. It took a few weeks, but when I finally saw Lake, it was clear he wasn't well.

Though the previous months had brought hope he could play baseball that spring, Lake's health continued to deteriorate. I don't know how much he actually played that season, if at all, but a few times, I would see Lake and his mom walking around the fields during practices. On one such occasion, I happened to be on a field running a practice with my team, and I saw them. I don't know why, but for some reason, I felt compelled to talk to him. I stopped what I was doing and walked to where they were. When I got there, I could see that Lake was struggling. I didn't know what to say but greeted them. He smiled tiredly, and it was clear he didn't have the energy to hold a conversation. Instead, I dropped to a knee and gently hugged his little body with one arm. I told him I loved him, that he was a great inspiration to me, and that I was praying for him. He and his mom smiled, thanked me, and we went our separate ways.

You may have read those last couple of sentences and found them odd. What business does a 40+-year-old man have telling a young child he hardly knows that he loves him? Some might find that awkward or even inappropriate. While it's true I was under a wellspring of emotion, I know I was also being guided by something beyond myself. In that moment, I wanted only to convey to another human how much I cared about them and their struggle. In words, it came out as "I love you," which, although perhaps awkward given our lack of formal relationship, was wholly accurate and genuine. I didn't regret saying it then, and as long as I live, I never will. In fact, the lack of regret or shame for love is another gift I can thank Lake for revealing to me.

Today, I am freer with those words than ever. More and more often, they are the last words I say to someone as we part company or end a conversation. Don't get me wrong – I'm not routinely professing my love for the Amazon delivery guy or random strangers at the dog park. But for those I know, with whom I have built relationships and in whom I am emotionally invested? Absolutely. Imagine how different the world would be if most people were simply unafraid to acknowledge that we genuinely care about each other. Imagine how much more encouraged and fuller your heart would be if more of your conversations ended with "I love you." Years later, I can tell you from experience, the effect is significant.

There is another important reason I'll absolutely never regret expressing my feelings that day. I think it was the last time I saw Lake Bozman in person.

A few weeks later, in February, Lake got an infection, which escalated into septic shock and ultimately did major damage to his heart. He would not return to the baseball field, but he wasn't done making a life-changing impact, not even close.

Angels on Earth

In all of this, I've yet to introduce you to another person who is an absolute Angel of Appreciation. Lake's mother, Anna, is one of the kindest, most loving, and faithful people I've ever met. She's also hands-down, one of the strongest. One of the uniquely strange and potentially wonderful things about living in the age of social media is that it allows you to develop some level of "relationship" with people you only know tangentially or superficially. Through our many shared contacts in baseball, Anna and I became connected on social media. There, more so than in face-to-face life, I would come to experience the absolute fullness with which Anna was purposefully pouring every ounce of her energy into making the most of every moment she had with Lake. A lot of it was the "small stuff" of life that all of our social profiles include. Some of it was massive, though, like the night in April of 2015, when Lake got the opportunity to live out a lifelong athletic dream. The Atlanta Hawks of the National Basketball Association officially signed Lake Bozman to a one-day contract, hosting him and his family for a special celebration during one of the team's home games. I still get emotional thinking about the joy this once-in-a-lifetime experience, one created mainly by the kindness of strangers, must have brought Lake and his family. The awesomeness of that dream coming true for him aside, there's something about being part of a team that changes the dynamics of the struggles we would otherwise face alone — more on that in a moment.

Big or small, each of these moments Anna captured and shared was building connective tissue in my emotional investment in this child, as I saw the rise and fall of his battle with a disease I so desperately hated.

I realize now that a lot of that investment was in not just Lake but in his family as a whole – particularly Anna. Only in hindsight can I see how watching his journey play out, even though the semi-removed lens of social media, awakened parts of my own experience with Kim's passing that I failed to recognize for a long time. What I got to see from Anna – selfless devotion to her child, with energy and faith that knew no limits – was what I think I initially missed seeing in the dynamic between Kim and my parents. Please, understand me here. I'm not suggesting at all that my parents didn't do exactly the same for my sister. I'm saying they DID and that I just didn't SEE it. During a lot of Kim's journey, I was 19 years old, 200 miles away, and making decisions that made me just as distant mentally, emotionally, and spiritually. Between my immaturity, my geography, and my anger, I wasn't there to see how they loved her, supported her, fought with and for her, celebrated her triumphs, and worried and prayed over her setbacks. It's not even that I didn't know on some fundamental level that all of that was happening; it's that I just didn't, or couldn't, think about it at the time.

Fast forward 30 years. Add years of healing to replace the anger. Add the birth of my own two children to provide the context of parenthood. And add in technology that allows the unlimited sharing of our every activity and feeling, which allowed me to see Lake's journey, and Anna's alongside him. A whole new appreciation for my parents' experience of losing a child to cancer emerges with crystal clarity. I don't think the gift of this realization is something I've thanked Anna, or apologized to my parents for, yet – which are opportunities I'm very much looking forward to Appreciating.

And a Child Shall Lead Them

Those gifts aren't the only ones Lake gave me either. I mentioned the crisis of faith I suffered after Kim's passing. I was certain God's seeming rebuke of my prayers for her health was a deal-breaker, and I had been willing to walk away from Him. In Lake, I saw a degree of faith that may only be possible for children – those without the burden of years of accumulated doubts, disappointments, and cynicism. In Anna, I saw something perhaps even more remarkable – the same strong faith in adulthood, even WITH those added weights.

In Luke 18:17, we're told: *"Truly, I say to you, whoever does not receive the kingdom of God like a child shall not enter it."* That's Lake for sure, but it's not the Scripture I most associate with him. For that, I'll direct you to 2 Corinthians 5:7.

In a section often headed as "Awaiting the New Body," Chapter 5 begins:

"For we know that if the earthly tent we live in is destroyed, we have a building from God, an eternal house in heaven, not built by human hands. 2 Meanwhile we groan, longing to be clothed instead with our heavenly dwelling, 3 because when we are clothed, we will not be found naked. 4 For while we are in this tent, we groan and are burdened, because we do not wish to be unclothed but to be clothed instead with our heavenly dwelling, so that what is mortal may be swallowed up by life. 5 Now the one who has fashioned us for this very purpose is God, who has given us the Spirit as a deposit, guaranteeing what is to come. 6 Therefore we are always confident and know that as long as we are at home in the body we are away from the Lord."

And then finally, 2 Corinthians 5:7

"7 For we live by faith, not by sight."

In the one simple line of this last verse is the directive that fueled Lake's fight. There was always steadfast, seemingly unshakeable faith. Not just in the doctors, treatments, friends or family that he could SEE supporting him, but real Faith in the Unseen One that Lake knew was holding him, regardless of his worldly circumstances. Faith like that is uncommon, and remarkable, and a gift.

To live by faith, and not by sight is perhaps the Truth I struggle with most often. It's a lesson Lake Bozman has been trying to teach me almost since the day we met. I'm *still* working on it, but I *am* still *working* on it.

Banded Together

In that spring baseball season of 2015, the one he would start but not finish, Lake added a teaching aid to my lesson that would become an enduring symbol and constant reminder.

As that season began, Lake had every intention of playing. But it quickly became apparent that he simply would not physically be able to. True to form, that didn't stop him. It didn't stop him from coming to practice when he could, to watch. It didn't stop him from coming to cheer on his friends. It didn't stop him from being part of their team. And pretty soon, we'd ALL be invited to join HIS team.

Remember, Lake had been fighting his battle for years at this point. There were already A LOT of people in his corner fighting with him. To show support, the family had created red rubber wristbands with the words "Team Lake" and that verse "2 Corinthians 5:7" stamped into them. I'd seen the bands on both Lake and Anna, and I'm sure if I had been paying attention, I would have seen several others already throughout the ballpark, but I hadn't connected the dots.

One Saturday morning, as we were preparing our teams to play, our league's commissioner approached me. He was carrying a bag containing several red wristbands. He explained that the family was inviting every coach and player to join TEAM LAKE and asked that I share the bands with our team. Talk about a double-edged sword.

On the one hand, it's an absolute no-brainer – of course, we would do that, and gladly. What a simple yet awesome way to show solidarity. On the other hand, I was instantly uncomfortable. Here was an opportunity to celebrate and honor a child, and one I was particularly fond of no less. So, what could possibly be the problem? Me. For just a moment, I let that request be about "me." I thought about being asked to speak publicly (not my favorite task), about cancer (certainly among my least favorite topics), to a group of eight-year-old kids. At that moment, I was terrified.

Thankfully, the moment, along with my selfish thoughts, passed quickly enough. What came of that opportunity was a real blessing. Before we took the field that day, we gathered our team of kids for just a minute. We gave them each a wristband – which, given they were 7 and 8 years old, we probably should have saved until the end, so they didn't play with them or get distracted. But then we talked. We talked about what it meant to be part of a team and how even though they were on a team together as baseball players, this wasn't the only one. Families are a team. Churches are a team. Classes are a team. And the great thing about being on a team is that it means you don't have to and *aren't supposed to* do everything yourself. When you do well, the whole team benefits. But when you struggle, or fail, or need help, the rest of the team is there to pick you up. Then we told them about Lake, how there was a boy in our league – a boy just like them – who was struggling. He was sick and fighting a pretty big battle. It didn't matter that he wasn't on our baseball team because he was on our LIFE team, and we were gonna be there to support him and pick him up.

Again, these kids were 7-8 years old. I don't know how much any of that registered or resonated with them that day. They loved the wristbands, though, and gleefully wore them that day and for the rest of the season. I also don't know that I even caught the lesson for myself in real-time. Only upon reflection do I realize I was basically re-sharing with those kids the same advice my wise old friends gave me at my sister's funeral many years ago. "(Let's make sure) He's not alone."

The season went on, and like most seasons, I couldn't tell you how many games our team won or lost. Though I certainly didn't think about Lake all the time, on my right wrist was a constant reminder that there were more important things in life than what happened on a baseball field.

A Broken Heart

May 1st, 2015 is a day I will never forget. It was a Friday morning. I was working from home in an empty house, and it was quiet. The phone rang. A voice I didn't recognize said my name. It was the coach who had first told me about Lake, a man I had known for years but never spoken to on the phone. I didn't even have time to process who I was talking to before he spoke words that would shatter my world.

"Hey, Steven. I got a call from Anna Bozman. Lake passed away early this morning."

I think I stopped breathing. I know beyond uttering an instinctive "oh no," I couldn't speak. The coach added that he wanted to let me know personally because he knew I had grown closer to Lake's family in those recent months. The conversation didn't last long. There wasn't much else to say, nor did either of us really feel like talking. In absolute shock, I hung up the phone and burst into tears.

I don't mean that water pooled up in my eyes and streamed down my cheeks. I mean that something deep inside my soul felt like it broke, releasing a torrent of emotion unlike anything I had felt before – and it was instantaneous. Then, and for a long while afterward, I processed this simply as a physical and emotional response to grief. That's accurate in part, but again, upon reflection, there was something else there too.

In revisiting the full arc of my experiences with cancer, it occurs to me that in the wake of my sister's death, I had what was probably an expected reaction in real-time to that episode too. But it was very different from my response to Lake's passing. When I was 21 and grieving Kim, I tried simply to obliterate my feelings. I drank. I smoked. I hid. I did lots of things just not to think or feel. I basically put a bunch of anger and hurt into a bottle, stuffed a giant cork in it, and buried it in the backyard of my soul. Horror writers and crime investigators share a favorite phrase – "nothing stays buried forever"– and they're right. On the morning of May 1st,

2015, the cork popped out of that bottle and unleashed everything inside.

With Lake's death, I was mourning the loss of a nine-year-old boy, which is profoundly sad itself. But did I even know him well enough to hurt that bad? Maybe not. But in its own way, it didn't even matter. Lake's passing was the first time since my sister's that I was forced to deal emotionally with a death from cancer. His passing was like tearing a Band-Aid off a wound that, although tightly dressed for decades, was still very raw.

The emotional response came and went fairly quickly. Once I was physically exhausted from crying, it started to subside. The spiritual toll was something altogether different. I've mentioned my spiritual journey, and specifically the crisis of faith that came with my sister's death. That journey is in constant progress. In the twenty-some years between Kim and Lake passing, I became less *actively* angry with God. But to say that I had totally resolved those feelings, that's not even close to accurate.

Every aspect of my crisis of faith came rushing back – fast and furious. I was mad. I was hurt. Once again, my prayers seemingly unanswered, I felt abandoned and ignored by God. The fact that this newest loss was of such a young soul made it somehow worse. How in the world could God let THAT happen? Never fully reconciled from before, He and I were definitely not moving in the same direction here. And once again, I was missing signs and the ultimate path.

Now, I was sitting 0-2 in my prayers to save the lives of loved ones from cancer. I still had that red rubber bracelet on my wrist as a reminder, but I failed to see the simple directive of Lake's example. I was failing to live by faith, out of blindness from what I had seen with my own eyes. But even in that failure, there was an opportunity to appreciate the situation.

In much that same way that Lake's passing dredged up slumbering pain from my own sister's death, it awakened my senses in other ways too. I mentioned before about not being able to appreciate in real time what my parents had suffered when Kim died. That certainly changed with the added perspective of two decades. I also had failed to appreciate just how much WORK they had done in her honor and memory. At the time of Kim's passing, I was still in college and not living with my parents. I failed to appreciate how they made the transition from mourning Kim to memorializing her – a process that ultimately helps with healing. I knew now, though, that Anna and her family were about to have to make that same transition. Having not taken those same opportunities relative to my sister, I didn't want to make that mistake again.

Within a week of his passing, I had the honor of attending Lake Bozman's funeral. I wasn't part of Lake's family, and in truth, was only a recent friend. But I was so affected and inspired by his journey that I absolutely wanted to be part of celebrating his life that day. Like Kim's service so many years ago, I marveled at the sheer number of people in attendance. The sanctuary of the family's large church was full. Arriving just a few moments before the service began, I joined the very end of a line where Anna and the rest of Lake's family greeted guests as they came in. I searched my brain for words and found none. I was sad but also a little relieved when the family retreated to take their seats before I reached them. I'd have to wait to pay my respects properly, and honestly, that worked out just fine. The service was a wonderfully sweet celebration. And though a sad occasion, it was hard not to be uplifted and encouraged by so many people gathered together to honor Lake's life. I left that service with a mix of somberness and odd peace, and a sense there was more to be done.

Something Larger Than Ourselves

I didn't see or speak with Lake's family for a few months after that, but he was always on my mind. We finished that spring baseball season and started preparing for the summer all-star tournaments in which many of our boys participated. During our times together as coaches and parents, there would sometimes be mentions of Lake. Some simply lamented the sadness of his passing. Some asked if anyone knew how his family was doing. A few people wondered if there was something we could do collectively as a baseball family and community to show our support. That notion threw my brain into a completely different gear.

Having coached there for years, I knew the people who were in leadership positions at the park. They are all kind, decent, loving people with big hearts for God and the kids who play baseball in their community. So, when approached with the prospect of finding a formal way to honor Lake, they were certainly open to the idea. We discussed several possibilities and eventually landed on creating a special award to be given in his name. Park leadership asked if I would share the idea with Anna. I was honored to do so, and with her blessing, we established the Lake Bozman Award.

From that point forward, each spring, Mount Paran North baseball would celebrate Lake's remarkable spirit by recognizing the player in each age group who best demonstrated those same qualities as they played the game of baseball. I was asked to describe in words those qualities and, thus, the spirit of the award.

As I thought about that, I revisited the conversation we had with the players a few months earlier, when we first introduced the Team Lake wristbands. I recalled that in addition to just explaining what those wristbands represented and meant, we also issued a challenge to our players. We talked in terms of Lake fighting a battle, but also the importance of HOW you fight. We talked about what it looks like to *win* a fight, even if that win doesn't show up on the scoreboard or the standings. We asked them to let those wristbands remind them that every time they took the field, they should want to fight with the same resolution and class that Lake brought to a much bigger and more important battle. With that as a frame of reference, the following description was crafted:

The Lake Bozman Award will be given to a player who competes with character and integrity, meets adversity with faith and positivity, and never gives up. This player sees every challenge as an opportunity to experience and share in the joy of being part of God's great plan and being part of something larger than ourselves. This player should also exemplify a positive spirit, perseverance, and playing the game of baseball with exceptional character, joy, or inspiration.

Take baseball out of the above scenario entirely. What remains is still a pretty good prescription for how to approach most of life's endeavors. The exercise of trying to articulate what I found so inspiring about Lake is an opportunity I genuinely appreciated – then and now. As of this writing, I am 48 years old, and I'll be frank with you – I STILL can't claim to have the same degree of faith that Lake Bozman already did at nine. I can tell you a few things I do have, though.

Five years after Lake's passing, I still have that same red rubber bracelet on my right wrist. I look at it every day and think not only about the boy it honors but also about the invaluable gifts of wisdom and context his life has brought to mine. I think about the relationships that I have today and realize that while a few of them are direct products of having known Lake, ALL of them are positively influenced by the huge impact that little boy made on my heart. Perhaps the thing I love, and yes, appreciate the most is the degree to which that impact has spread. I don't know where all of the kids from my Spring 2015 baseball team are today, but I'm happy beyond words to say that wasn't the last group of kids who have worn those wristbands. Best of all, some of them are still on Team Lake today.

My youngest son, the one just a few months away in age from Lake, also still wears that wristband every day. He would later play with a travel baseball team made up of boys from this same park, all of whom were also contemporaries, teammates of, or competitors with Lake. The core of that team would stay together for another four years, ultimately ending their run together at the youth baseball Mecca that is Cooperstown Dreams Park.

I talked to Anna before our team left for that trip. Over those years, we'd grown closer, and she knew that because of the relationships we'd built, our team, in particular, had continued to carry Lake in our hearts. We talked about how given their ages, this was the year Lake would have also had the chance to go to Cooperstown. I wanted to make sure she knew that if we were going, he would be there too.

When our team arrived in upstate New York to compete against 110 other teams from across the country, they did so with Team Lake stickers on their batting helmets and each wearing a red wristband. We also committed to donating to Lake's cancer research fund for every home run we hit that week – we got 10. With every trip our boys took around those bases, I looked up and smiled, appreciating every second of it. As of this writing, that trip was more than a year ago. Most of those boys have gone their separate ways, though we still try to keep that 'family' together when we can. A couple of the other boys from that team are still wearing their Team Lake bands years later too. They're young enough to still lose and break stuff pretty regularly. So, every so often, I'll get a text from one of those kids saying, "Hey Coach. I lost my Lake band. Can you get me another one?" My heart smiles as I tell them, "of course." That usually means that I have to go back to Anna and see if she can send me a few more wristbands. I don't mind, though, and I'm guessing she probably doesn't either.

Writing these essays is a bit of a surreal experience. Before I sat down to put all these memories into words, I had no sense of just how much the act of revisiting them would reveal to me and what I would learn. With every day, I'm increasingly grateful for the lessons Lake Bozman has taught me and for every new opportunity I get to apply them.

✳✳✳

I wish I could tell you that my next break in between the hard lessons of cancer would last as long as the one between Kim's passing and Lake's. If that were the case, I'd still be blissfully ignorant of some other painful truths. Sadly, my next lesson was waiting right around the corner – literally.

Just down the street from us, and around that corner, lived my friend, Kevin. He and his wife Jackie were a couple of years younger, but their family was very much like ours. Their two kids were the same ages as ours; we served on school boards and attended neighborhood events together; we spent nights at each other's homes playing games, watching football, and just hanging out. In short, they were part of the Tribe that Carie and I had been "doing life with" for years.

In the fall of 2014, Kevin went to the doctor, concerned about persistent pain in his abdomen. That September, he would be shocked to learn that testing revealed tumors in his gastrointestinal tract. Those tumors would turn out to be malignant, and Kevin's doctor referred him to specialists at MD Anderson Medical Center in Houston, TX, for consultation and care.

In reading just this much so far, you may have noticed some overlap in the timing of Lake and Kevin's battles. I don't think I properly processed this in real time. But, in hindsight, it turns out to be significant. I had been friends with Kevin for years and was aware of his diagnosis before I think I had even met Lake Bozman. I mention that as a way of linking the two of them together. The truth is, they never met. Their only connection to each other was that I knew them both, but in my world, the interplay of their cases would end up, years later, revealing something crucial I had never previously understood.

Given the relative rarity and complexity of his case, Kevin's treatment was less straightforward, too. There were plenty of unknowns, but Carie and I were absolutely invested emotionally in our friend and his family's well being. As his case progressed, more information became available about Kevin's condition and his prognosis. If anything, as we learned that things might not be moving in the right direction for him, our levels of concern and emotional investment increased, as you would expect. Then, something unexpected and awful happened.

In May of 2015, when Lake passed away, something snapped in my soul. Decades of bottled-up pain and fear about Kim came rushing back. I probably knew in real time the result of that was not going to be good. I know now, unfortunately, it was even worse than I thought. The other thing that returned with the passing of Lake was my crisis of faith. With his death, I doubled down on the belief that God didn't hear, or worse yet, simply wasn't interested in responding to my prayers on the specific subject of helping my loved ones overcome cancer.

Sadly, when your default is cynicism, it always seems to sit right at or just under the surface, waiting to rear its ugly head. And it did. I wish I could say I was mentally or emotionally stronger. But in that particular season – when my friend likely needed it the most – I was utterly empty.

Mark 12:31 commands us to *"love thy neighbor as thyself."* So, what happens when your literal neighbor needs love more than ever, and you yourself are in an awful place? In my case, what happens is not good. Sadly, I have to admit that in the very time I could have been the most helpful, most reassuring, most comforting, most neighborly, and most loving to my friend in need, I failed comprehensively. There's another well-worn saying that suggests, "you can't give what you don't have." Looking back, that's precisely where I was.

The Empty Cup

There was something I couldn't give in that situation because there was something I didn't have. In the wake of Lake's passing, even with that red rubber band on my wrist as a reminder and his enduring example as an encouragement, somehow, what I didn't have was faith. As terrible as it sounds, and again, I'm embarrassed to admit it now, deep down, I didn't really believe everything was going to be okay.

Don't get me wrong. It's not that I walked away or even withdrew. We saw Kevin and Jackie pretty regularly. We were around and available. I still cared and still loved him. But I was seriously lacking. I lacked faith, and I lacked hope. And that ultimately meant I was poorly-equipped to help my friends.

Here, I want to make something else clear. It's also not that I didn't even pray for this situation. I did, and kind of often, too. But those prayers lacked any real conviction, and thus probably any real power because they were essentially faithless prayers. It turns out, God has something to say about that.

James 1:6 says: *"But when you ask, you must believe and not doubt, because the one who doubts is like a wave of the sea, blown and tossed by the wind."* And in Hebrews 11:6, we hear: *"God is a rewarder of them who seek Him."*

I must admit, I wasn't. I was praying to a God who I'd been keeping at arm's length because I'd decided He didn't want me to have what I was praying for. That's a terrible place to be, and I stayed there far too long. For months, Kevin soldiered on, returning to Houston periodically for checkups and treatments. He'd have good and bad days but somehow always maintained that wide trademark smile of his. I'd see him most often at the bus stop as we dropped off or picked up our kids, and we'd talk. In between bits about college football, our kids' activities, or goings-on in the neighborhood, he'd give me updates on his treatments and how he felt. I listened and gave what encouragement I could, which I wish was so much more.

That summer, we joined Kevin and Jackie's family on a beach trip to Hilton Head, SC, a place both our families love but had not previously enjoyed together. Kevin wasn't feeling great, but he was in good spirits. For the trip, he'd splurged on a Bucket List item and rented a beautiful convertible Corvette, which during that vacation became a literal vehicle for him and his family to take joy rides.

I'm not a 'car guy,' but man, that thing was cool. Kevin drove from Atlanta to Hilton Head with his son in that car and planned to have his daughter join him in it on the return. As is often the case, life threw a curveball. Based on one of his tests, it turned out Kevin needed to go back a day or two early to start a new treatment. The girls decided to keep the kids at the beach, and I ended up riding back with Kevin to Atlanta in that Corvette. That's a decision I'll appreciate forever. He never let me drive that car, but that was perfectly fine. I had the best seat imaginable. The ride was cool, but the company was way better. For five straight hours, we talked and laughed, so much so that when I got home, my face hurt from smiling. In many ways, that five-hour ride was a microcosm of our relationship. He was the one suffering, but you wouldn't know it. Kevin had a capacity for joy that is rare, and it was infectious. I was probably the one who should have been working hard to make him happy, but he was the one doing that for me and making it look effortless. That joy, that trademark smile, those things are timeless, even if we're not.

By August, not long after that beach trip, Kevin's body stopped responding to the treatments. On August 10th, 2016, with his wife and their two kids by his side, Kevin passed away. Like all his many other friends, Carie and I were devastated by the news. The emotions came as they had in the past – sadness, frustration, anger, helplessness, etc. But somehow, this time, it was different for me.

Don't Wait. Say It All Now!

When Kim passed, I was completely naïve. I had never experienced the death of a close loved one, and even despite that doctor's stark admission, I don't think I thought it was really going to happen until it did. When Lake passed, I was in denial. I knew such a thing was possible, but I still wanted to believe God wasn't going to *let* that happen. With Kevin, sadly, I don't think either of those things is true. I wasn't naïve about the gravity of his condition. I also wasn't in denial about the possible outcome, and even sadder, I don't think I was relying on God to intervene. I think I knew that beach trip and that Corvette joy ride would be "forever" memories. Please understand. If there is any upside at all to that kind of sad clarity, it's that it creates a sense of hyper-awareness and mindfulness. When you recognize those moments as they're happening, there's a conscious effort to hit "record" in your brain – to be extra present; to miss nothing, and remember everything. That's good and terrible at the same time.

Why is it bad? Because it reveals the degree to which we – or at least I – don't live like that ALL the time. We shouldn't need the prospect of our time with someone we care about ending to be mindful about appreciating every minute of it that we have. And similarly, we shouldn't wait until we hear the clock ticking, or God forbid after it runs out, to tell people how we feel about them and what they mean to us. In a very specific way, this is the other lesson Kevin's passing would teach me.

Shortly after Kevin passed, as their family was preparing for his memorial service, I got a phone call. It was Jackie. She was calling to ask if I would be willing to speak at Kevin's funeral. I was caught completely off-guard. Of course, we were friends and had been close for years, but it honestly never occurred to me that such a request, such an honor really, would come to me. That's another one that should be a no-brainer. Any normal person in that situation would say, "yes, of course, it would be an honor," and that would be that.

So, what was my response? Just like I did when asked to talk to those young baseball players about Lake – I hesitated, and I froze. Somehow, at that moment, my ridiculous brain succumbed again to its cynical and selfish defaults. In that moment of panic, I actually told my friend that I wasn't sure if I could do it; I wasn't sure I was the right person for that job. I asked her if I could "think about it" and get back to her. Seriously? Your friend's widow, who is also your friend, calls and asks you to speak at his funeral, and you want to "think about it?" Not cool, dude. Not cool at all.

As I hung up the phone, I already knew several things INSTANTLY. I knew I had handled that awfully. I knew *why* I had balked – entirely out of fear. I knew I was afraid of public speaking. I knew I was scared to stand in front of people and talk about losing a friend. I knew I was terrified to "get it wrong" or look foolish. Worst of all, I knew I was afraid to admit that on some perverse level, I didn't appreciate being put in that situation. Thankfully, there was something else I also knew instantly.

Through all the noise and anxiety that had just exploded in my brain, I knew there was no way I was going to say no to that request. It took me a minute, during which you'll be completely unsurprised that I turned to Carie for counsel, but I did call Jackie back and tell her it would be my honor to speak at the service. In that return call, I think I thanked her for asking me, but to this day, I'm not sure I've fully thanked her yet for what that experience has taught me. So, let me try again.

I'm a writer by nature and vocation. I've been doing it professionally for decades. In that time, I've written all kinds of things: essays, poems, a novel, scripts, and more than a million words of advertising and marketing copy. One thing I had never written, or even thought about writing, before Jackie's call, was a eulogy. What a curiously heavy and challenging exercise - to capture the essence of a person's life in words. But what a tremendous opportunity as well. How do you accurately convey a person's spirit, their impact, or what they mean to you? The answer is, you spend a lot of time thinking about those very things. The specific words become much less important than the sentiments they convey. What you hope for are authenticity and sincerity. If you get those things right, you're probably going to be okay.

I did spend a lot of time thinking, but it didn't take me long to recognize that the essence of my friend's life was Joy. In big and small ways, he was good at creating it, sharing it, and living in it. As difficult as it is to write about someone's life, it was easy to describe the many ways Kevin embodied and demonstrated joy – and yes, that Corvette definitely got a mention too.

Writing a eulogy wasn't what I feared – that was just me vs. a blank page, working to find and assemble words; I can do that. What terrified me was the prospect of standing before people and delivering it. I've described noticing the volume of attendance at both Kim and Lake's funerals. In both those instances, I appreciated how many people had come to pay their respects. Kevin's was very similar. As I watched that large church sanctuary fill with people, I got very nervous. But then, I remembered why we were there in the first place. We were there to celebrate his life. And even though it was a sad occasion, I was armed with a happy story about a wonderful man whose life was a testament to joy. There's no time or space for fear there.

I stood before those people and shared that happy story. I stuck close to my page or two of notes and only spoke for a couple of minutes. Before I knew it, I was finished. I returned to my seat and listened to the rest of the service with my family. While I sat there, though, I had a realization. The fact that I had a lump in my throat and a flushed face didn't surprise me, but the specific reason for the emotions I was feeling at that moment did. What I realized is what an overwhelming experience it is to stand in front of people and express gratitude and love for another person. What a great honor it is to stand in public and tell someone that their husband, or father, or friend was a good person whose life positively impacted your own. That's powerful stuff and a great lesson learned. But there's something even more powerful, a way to Appreciate that lesson even further.

Writing and sharing Kevin's eulogy introduced me to the experience of sharing how I felt about someone I had known, cared about, and lost. But because I was delivering those words as a eulogy, I was sharing those thoughts about him with everyone EXCEPT him at his funeral. What a colossal, missed opportunity.

Why do we wait until people are gone to say all the nice things we've known about them for so long? Is it because we don't spend the time even thinking about those things until the time comes to pay our respects? Or is it because we're afraid to be vulnerable with our feelings? Either way, it's a huge miss.

In the same way that Lake created a freeness in me to simply share the sentiment of loving another person, regardless of my level of relationship with them, Kevin showed me the importance of not waiting until it's too late to tell people what they mean to us.

That got me thinking, and this might sound odd, or even a bit morbid, but what if we went through the exercise of "writing eulogies" for all the important people in our lives – while they're still here? What if we sat and thought about the qualities that defined them and the "forever" memories that will define our relationships with those people? And then, what if we shared that with each other? Imagine if someone came to you and said, "you know, I've always loved (this) about you. I'll never forget when we went to (this place) and did those things. I'm so grateful you were with me when (this happened). My life is fuller, and my world is a better place because you're in it." Do you think you would appreciate that? I know I would.

✳✳✳

So now, you've met three people in my life who have fought cancer. You've probably also noticed that in my attempts to pray for those people – for their healing and their very survival, I went 0-3. Even if you weren't a cynical pessimist by default, that might be hard to overcome.

I want to introduce you to one more person. His name is also Kevin, which isn't necessarily ironic but is somehow appropriate here. This "second" Kevin is another friend of mine and is a fellow parishioner at our church. We met there several years ago, as a function of us both having young kids and me working at the check-in desk for children's church on Sunday mornings. At first, our "relationship" was based almost entirely on our shared love for the University of South Carolina and its less than stellar sports teams. While that road alone is often enough to make a person cynical, I would soon discover that this Kevin was anything but.

Aside from their names and being my friend, the thing these two Kevins had most in common was their capacity for positivity. In the first Kevin's case, that positivity registered as Joy, an outward expression of happiness, even in situations where it might be surprising or unexpected. In the second Kevin, it's something a little different, which I'll get to momentarily.

Over the last few years, I've gotten to know this second Kevin on a much deeper level. We still revel in Gamecock wins and commiserate in their defeats, but there's a lot more there now. And honestly, a big part of what's there now is the most significant thing that was missing for me as I went through my experiences with Kim, Lake, and my other friend Kevin. What's there now is a closeness to God that is unprecedented in my life, and even better, a willingness to draw closer still. In the strangest way, I have this Kevin, and cancer, to 'thank' for that.

For years, we only saw church Kevin and his family in passing on Sunday mornings. I'd talk to him for a couple of minutes about his kids or Gamecock football or baseball, and we'd go our separate ways. Our kids were in different school situations, we didn't live near each other, and we were in different small groups at church, so those few minutes each week were our only intersection. Sometimes though, a few minutes is all you need with someone to know they are one of "your people." By that, I don't even mean that we have a ton in common. As I would find out as we got to know each other better, we have very different experiences and have led pretty different lives, but there's still a kindred spirit there that's easy to recognize.

Fast forward a few more years. The small group that Carie and I had been a part of for years had sort of naturally dissolved, and while we still loved and occasionally saw those folks, the fact we were no longer meeting regularly left us missing a sense of community. A year or two went by without us being part of any such group. That was okay for a while, but both Carie and I recognized that something was missing. The spirit of community, and the active practice of "doing life together" with people in a similar place, have a value that I probably can't overstate.

When we realized Kevin and his family were part of a small group that also included other people at the church we knew and enjoyed, we approached them to see if there was an opportunity for us to join them. They were open to the idea and invited us to visit, which turned out to be another serendipitous decision.

It's been a couple of years now since we started attending that group, and what a blessing it has been and continues to be. Immediately, a few things were evident to me about this particular group. First, they were all very close. They'd been together for years and had developed deep relationships with each other, of which Carie and I were not yet really a part. They also were all deeply spiritual, with an undeniable sense of clarity and certainty around their faith. Those two things probably combined to create a third reality, which is that they were remarkably open. I mean this both in general and specific. They were open to a new family joining their tight circle. They were open to sharing their successes and blessings, and more importantly, they were open to sharing their challenges, shortcomings, and struggles. In this particular group, each among them was certain that all of those blessings came from God and their obedience to His desires for them. They were equally sure that God's provision was more than ample to overcome their struggles. I know in my heart that Carie was already living that way, too. And then there was me. I'd walked away entirely from God in my twenties after Kim died. Since then, I'd managed to at least turn back around, and I would occasionally take timid baby steps in the right direction. But then, trauma or tragedy would strike again, my faith would take another ding, and I would shut down. Rinse and repeat.

I would say I was "trying," but the truth is, I was unconvinced. More accurately, I was conflicted. I had become much more comfortable with the idea that God was indeed involved in, if not wholly responsible for, my blessings. I'd seen enough things happen that I couldn't explain any other way. But I still wasn't buying the other half of that equation. I was still holding tightly to the notion that God wasn't particularly interested in hearing or answering certain prayers of mine. He seemed to be holding out on me, and there was part of me that was perfectly willing to reciprocate. That's not a great place to be. It can actually be pretty uncomfortable being the lone grudge-holding cynic in a room full of friends who are not. And sometimes, that's a good thing. Most good things happen when we get a little uncomfortable.

It's kind of fun going around a circle and sharing with friends about the good things that are happening in your life. That new job? Praise God! Closed on a house? Amen! Unsurprisingly, it's easy to have faith when everything is going well. But what happens when the coin lands on the other side, or we draw the short stick? I know what *my* typical response is. *"I don't appreciate that."* This group, and Kevin, were about to show me a different way.

Much of this book is me sharing events from my distant past and relaying how time and hindsight have changed my perspective. Here, I get to deal in near real time.

We had been part of this small group for over a year. During that time, there had been plenty of sharing. Each week, we'd all have the opportunity to give praise for our blessings and request prayer for our challenges. Often those events were the ups and downs of everyday life. But then, one week, our friend Kevin came to the group with something much more significant to share.

In July of 2020, in response to inexplicable discomfort, Kevin had gone to the doctor. Scans and testing ultimately revealed that he had testicular cancer. As that news settled across our group, you might expect the air to get heavy, filled with worry or fear or doubt. I know I personally had all of those feelings. My cynical brain went into its default mode and started telling me things like, *"Well, here we go again."* While the instinct to pray for his healing kicked in, it was equaled by doubt. *"We've been here before,"* my brain said. *"You know how this goes – how it ALWAYS goes."* No matter how you slice it, that's awful. Once again, as a friend is in need, I felt paralyzed by doubt. *"This hasn't worked before. Why would it be any different this time?"* Man, that negative voice in my head can be loud and persistent.

But something was different here. Imagine a flame. Without oxygen and fuel, even a raging fire gets extinguished. What it needs to prosper, and spread, is to be fed. So, there I am, alone in my doubt, surrounded by the one thing that absolutely refuses to feed fear – faith.

Remember a little while ago when I said that my two Kevins shared a sense of positivity? In this Kevin, that positivity is nearly overwhelming, in a great way. The minor, understandable cynicism that comes from pulling for the Gamecocks aside, Kevin is probably one of the happiest, most positive people I know. And it's not even the kind of "happy" that comes from mere contentment. Nor is it the enjoyment of a life of ease, devoid of difficulty. He's known plenty of struggle. And yet, there's almost a radiance to him. What I know now is that's the light of faith shining outwardly from within him. And here's the thing, every other person in this small group has the same shine.

Back to the flame. My brain hears familiar bad news; cue the pilot light. That flame of doubt comes alive. But now, that flame is surrounded by an energy it simply can't burn. Turn back to those verses we looked at earlier. I was stuck living the back (wrong) half of James 1:6 *"But when you ask, you must believe and not doubt... because the one who doubts is like a wave of the sea, blown and tossed by the wind."* Meanwhile, everyone else around me is living the other, right half.

The other thing that was remarkable to me in this situation was the immediacy, strength, and certainty with which Kevin and the rest of the group met this challenge head-on. Even the prayers themselves were different. In Philippians 4:6, we get this:

"Do not be anxious or worried about anything, but in everything [every circumstance and situation] by prayer and petition with thanksgiving, continue to make your [specific] requests known to God."

They were praying, but it was almost as if they weren't making a *request*. Our friends were proclaiming Kevin's health. Instead of asking that God DO something, they were TELLING God "thank you" for what He had ALREADY done. Immediacy. Strength. Certainty. That isn't a description of how they were practicing faith; that IS Faith.

Now go back to Hebrews 11:6. *"God is a rewarder of them who seek Him."*

Two weeks later, our friend Kevin had surgery to remove the tumor and other compromised tissue. With the same certainty, he and his family, and so many others around him, awaited confirmation of success. Three weeks after that, on August 6th, Kevin's follow-up appointment generated the news for which everyone prayed. He was clear of cancer. Amen, indeed!

Here's the thing. God is a mystery, and try as we might, we will always fall short of both His glory and the ability to understand His ways. I don't mean to suggest that there was something in this Kevin – something more worthy of His rescue – than in my other friend Kevin, or in Lake, or Kim. In every one of those situations, those people, and many around them had faith every bit as strong. One day, when I finally meet God, I'm sure the mystery of those outcomes, and many others, will be revealed. But for now, I'm grateful to an extent far beyond what I previously thought possible for the lessons my experiences with cancer have provided.

At the beginning of that journey, I had no experience, no knowledge, and no tools. Now, decades later, I have all of that and more. I would still tell you that I hate cancer. But in the oddest of ways, it's almost as if I should be thanking my enemy for all things it taught me and even some gifts I have received along the way.

Through my experience with Kim, I've seen sides of my parents I would never have outside of that struggle. I learned what it looks like to be a husband. And through Dennis' future marriage – serendipitously to one of Kim's best friends – I got two nephews and a niece that wouldn't even exist as the uniquely awesome people they are. Thank you.

Through my experience with Lake, I learned how love for others could and should transcend traditional relationships. I saw the power of child-like faith and had the opportunity to help connect others in honoring a legacy that embodies how we all should strive to live. Thank you.

Through my first friend Kevin, came the revelation of the depth of my brokenness. It also revealed the importance of living not only in the moment, with joy, but also with the freedom to express how important other people are in our lives. Thank you.

Through my second friend Kevin, I gained a bit of healing right along with him. I truly experienced what I had seen but not understood in my previous struggles – the remarkable difference abundant, overflowing faith can make. For once, and hopefully, for good, my cynicism was overwhelmed by a genuinely contagious certainty that still lingers in me. Thank you.

Across all these experiences spans one universal lesson. When Kim died, I felt utterly alone. Worse yet, I welcomed that solitude and even reveled in it. Then, in the experiences that followed, I wanted to be alone. Now I don't. Now, not that I ever want to face the specter of cancer again, I feel at least better equipped to handle things differently. For strength and guidance there, I'll look to another familiar verse:

Proverbs 17:17 – *"A friend loves at all times, but a brother is born for adversity."*

Cancer has shown me more adversity than just about anything else in this life. It's also revealed a couple of my strengths and many of my weaknesses in terms of being a friend. What I've come to embrace, and what I hope to be able to Appreciate moving forward, is the opportunity, strengthened by faith, to act as a true brother.

Questions to Consider:

• Even in the most profound times of loss or tragedy, there is wisdom and growth and love to appreciate. When has this been true in your life?

• What gifts might you possess that make you uniquely prepared to help someone else through the process of grief?

• Often, we think about how loss takes people away from our lives. Has there been an instance where a situation of loss has brought someone important into your life? What have you gained from that?

• Have you encountered a time when someone else's faith provided the light you needed to find the path to healing or help? Have you thanked them for that gift?

Wisdom to Appreciate:

Proverbs 17:17 – "A friend loves at all times, but a brother is born for adversity."

James 1:6 - "But when you ask, you must believe and not doubt, because the one who doubts is like a wave of the sea, blown and tossed by the wind."

Luke 18:17 - "Truly, I say to you, whoever does not receive the kingdom of God like a child shall not enter it."

2 Corinthians 5:7 - "For we live by faith, not by sight."

Chapter 4:
Appreciation at Work

When you meet someone for the first time – whether on a date, or the stranger sitting next to you on a plane, or anywhere else you're liable to engage in small talk – what's one of the first questions that's typically asked? "So, what do you DO?" There are alternate forms of this question. Often, it's "what do you do at work?" or even more commonly, "what do you do FOR A LIVING?" It's an easy conversation starter that can lead to some interesting places and reveal quite a bit about a person, depending on how they answer.

I've found that I answer that question very differently today than I did 20 years ago, or 10, or even 5. Mostly, I think that is because my understanding of the role my job plays in my overall identity continues to evolve over time. This is true for both how I see myself and how I present myself to others.

As much as some things evolve, there are constants too. For most of my life – even before I ever got paid to do it – if someone asked me, "what do you do?" somewhere in my answer would have been "I'm a writer." I guess I always have been, and I hope I always will be.

I was a weird kid in a lot of ways, including my designs for a career. Ask kids what they want to be when they grow up, and you'll get a variety of answers – everything from doctors and lawyers to astronauts, police officers, actors, and athletes. How many 12-year-olds are pretty sure they want to write advertisements? That's kind of weird, but that's me. And really, I don't even know why. At 12, the only person I knew of who was "in advertising" wasn't even real. Long before Don Draper enthralled viewers with a highly romanticized version of the advertising industry, there was Darren Stevens. Darren, the husband character on the 1970's television show *Bewitched,* was an ad man, but you never saw him actually DO any writing. So, aside from possibly all of the ads I watched on TV as a kid, I have no idea where the fascination came from initially.

I was also a voracious reader in my youth, tearing through everything from Tolkien to true crime stories, enjoying most of the classics assigned in school, and developing a minor obsession with Stephen King. I loved to read, and especially to discover new words, but at that age, the idea of writing novels was overwhelming. I was in awe of authors' abilities to conceive such complex narratives. Even if penning novels seemed unrealistic, I knew I wanted to be a writer in some form; I just didn't know how. And then I got some help.

By middle school, it was clear my brain didn't like math or science, but words were different. I understood words and knew how to put them together in ways that made sense and occasionally got noticed or praised. By the time I reached high school, there were precisely zero math teachers telling me that I had a talent for geometry, trigonometry, or calculus. But with English and composition teachers, I was finding real encouragement. Assignments to write essays or short stories were welcome challenges instead of drudgeries to be survived. I appreciated (with a small "a," and in the most general sense) the positive feedback I was getting from my writing efforts to that point. But this really just meant that it made me feel good that someone – anyone – happened to think I might be good at something.

As I started thinking about colleges and careers, the roads forked decidedly. Words and numbers were diverging paths, and I had all but written off the latter. When it came time to start trying to answer that "what (are you going) to do for a living" question for the first time – at the very mature age of 16 or 17 – like most of us, I wasn't prepared. My parents had a great plan, though – one I would end up Appreciating to this day.

I'm not sure how they knew about this, but my parents decided it would be a good idea to have my sister and me aptitude tested before sending us to college. Today, anyone with access to the Internet can log on and instantly find a plethora of tests that will claim to match you with your perfect career. Ironically, as a writer who has spent decades working in the super-specific realm of employment and recruitment advertising, I've even built a few of these tests myself.

Back in the late 1980s, there was, of course, no Internet. In those days, getting aptitude tested meant physically traveling to a corporate office and spending a full day working through a diverse battery of exams administered by several other humans. In retrospect, it seems a bit strange and clinical, but I have oddly positive memories of the experience.

The point of these tests was to evaluate one's proficiency on various tasks, each using different skills. They covered everything from math, logic, word association, memory games, vocabulary tests, and even musicality. In the end, they would rate your ability in all these areas and then arrive at a sliding scale inventory that showed the things you were very good at, all the way down to things at which you were objectively terrible. Then they cross-referenced your abilities with jobs that relied on those particular skills. What you walked away with was a basic personality overview and a detailed list of jobs that mapped directly to your skills. As I said, you can probably find some scaled-down version of this online for free in less than a minute right now – but as a high school student in 1988, the process seemed like absolute magic. I didn't understand the "science" behind it, and I certainly was in no position to appreciate it either. At the time, it was just something that my parents told me I was going to do.

So, what did the crystal ball tell me? Well, the bottom line was something like this: apparently, my brain has an even split in its analytical and abstract approach to problem solving. I have a high degree of creativity and a love-hate relationship with structure. I tend to thrive when I can apply myself to a range of different tasks, instead of getting bogged down in doing the same thing repetitively for an extended time. I need variety in the challenges I face to keep myself interested and motivated, and I also need the whip-crack of deadlines to keep me honest and productive. Words are my friends, numbers and musical notes, not so much.

I don't know how much you know about writing advertising, but if you were going to develop a profile of someone likely to succeed in that career, it might read a lot like that last paragraph. In fact, Advertising/Marketing Writer was near the top of a list of jobs these tests suggested I should pursue.

So, imagine being 16 or 17 years old. You're a year and a half away from college, and while you might have some idea about what you think you'd like to study, you're also close to clueless. Then, your parents come along and provide what feels like solid, "scientific evidence" that you might be naturally good at the thing that interests you. Imagine the boost in confidence this little extra layer of validation provides. Again, at the time, I don't think I knew how to appreciate the value of that gift of direction and assurance my parents gave me. But, I do know that after a few years in college (and certainly in the decades that followed), I saw plenty of people who were struggling even to find the path they were supposed to be on, let alone follow it to some successful destination. Believing I was headed in the right direction from the start and being told I was well-equipped to succeed made a huge difference in how I approached college entirely. I questioned plenty of things between the ages of 18-22, but the path of my professional pursuits was never one of them.

As of this writing, my children are 15 and 13. My oldest is a sophomore in high school. Am I determined to raise them exactly as my parents raised my sister and me? I'm not. But do I have every intention of giving them as many gifts of encouragement, direction, and validation as possible? Absolutely. Those are gifts I can only hope to Appreciate as much as they deserve to be.

You Can't Stay Here Forever

I shouldn't miss the opportunity to mention how much I appreciate my college experience. It's true in general, but most specifically, I mean the sacrifices my parents made to make that happen for my sister and me. As I mentioned earlier, my father went to college but didn't finish. My mother never went. I don't know that my sister and I gave it much thought at the time, but there was never really an alternate plan – we were *going* to college. For me, it changed everything. The academics completely aside, college was an opportunity for me to change my scenery, escape a difficult childhood, and literally start a new life in a new place where no one knew anything about me. That alone was worth the price of admission. And the relationships I developed during that time, many of which endure to this day, were among the most genuine and valuable friendships I've ever formed. In some ways, I didn't need college to "find a career" – I probably would have ended up pursuing more or less the same path either way. But I did manage to "find" some version of myself, which was just as valuable, if not more so.

As teenagers, we're incredibly self-centered creatures. At that age, I didn't spend much time thinking about what my college experience required of other people (my parents). Nor did I think much about my fellow students who were working their asses off while also going to classes to pay for their own education. Nor did it occur to me to consider all those who would have loved to have the opportunity I was taking too much for granted, but for whom college wasn't an option. Only as an adult could I see the sacrifices my parents made to make college possible for me. That's something I'll try to properly Appreciate for the rest of my life.

With my children quickly approaching the same crossroads, I think a lot about what all of this means, or can mean, for them.

There's a part of me that wants to give my children every advantage I had – and more if possible. This is a basic instinct for many parents. There's also a part of me that thinks I probably had it way too easy. Maybe if I had to struggle a little more, I might have discovered appreciation (for other peoples' generosity and my own self-reliance) sooner. My guess is my wife and I will split the difference as we parent our own children. Our boys are probably more aware of gratitude and empathy than I was at their age, which gives me hope that they can appreciate opportunity and challenge in equal measure.

I graduated from the University of South Carolina in 1995 with a degree in Advertising. But the end of that road was just the beginning of a life-long journey of trying to figure out what to DO next. My parents had been crucial in support of my education, but suddenly, things were different. By the age of 21, I had mastered the skill of NOT listening to my father – not because he wasn't a good dad; he was then, and still is – but because, like most young men trying to figure out life, I just didn't want to listen. So, I'm sure he said a lot of things back then I could have benefitted from if only I had listened with intent. But I do specifically recall two things he told me not long after my graduation.

The first was, "I'm proud of you, and I know you picked the right degree for your talents. I don't know anything about the industry you've chosen or anyone who works in it, so there's not much I can do to help you." That's a heart-warming sentiment that I both understood and appreciated.

The second was, "Your mom loves you very much. She would probably be fine with you coming back home to live with us forever. She and I agree on the first point, but not the second."

Ouch. I definitely didn't appreciate that. Here, "I don't appreciate that" translates roughly to "that's a painful truth I'd rather not acknowledge." There were more of those coming down the pike – several in fact, in quick succession.

Columbia, South Carolina is a lovely place. I haven't lived there since 1995, but a small piece of my soul still does. It has everything a small city should, including some of my favorite people as its residents. What it didn't have in 1995 was a lot of jobs in advertising. I made the rounds, circulating resumes and chasing a few fleeting opportunities after graduation, but nothing panned out. My parents let me linger for a few months but finally pulled the plug and brought me back to Atlanta to live in their basement. Pending homelessness aside, I didn't really appreciate that either.

Atlanta is a much bigger city than Columbia, with a lot more advertising agencies and jobs in general to pursue. I shotgun blasted resumes out and made cold calls for weeks, taking any appointment I could get. Still, that shiny dream job proved elusive. I lingered for a while, working jobs that had nothing at all to do with the degree I'd spent years getting. I took freelance writing jobs wherever I could find them. I did whatever I could to build contacts and catch a break.

At some point, I became aware there were a couple of "finishing" schools for advertising in the Atlanta area – places where creatives could practice their skills, working in pairs or teams on spec projects under the guidance of seasoned industry pros. It was like graduate school in that it costs money to attend, but different in that there was no advanced degree waiting for you at the end. What it did seem to promise was a near 100% placement rate for graduates. I managed to convince my parents that more school was the answer to my current lack of purposeful employment and enrolled at the burgeoning Creative Circus school of advertising in 1996. It was supposed to take students two years to complete the curriculum. I got about halfway there before everything changed again.

A few semesters into the program at The Creative Circus, I reached another crossroads. I was really enjoying my time there, doing good work, and spending time with some of the most fun and creative people I have ever met. I was also getting restless and a little nervous about accumulating student debt. One day, as I was walking down the main hallway, I passed by the Job Board. Remember, this was 1996-97, so I literally mean a physical bulletin board upon which potential job opportunities were pinned. I'd passed by that board countless times before without giving it much thought. For some reason, on that day, I stopped and did a little window shopping. I don't recall how many jobs there were for writers on that board, but I did see at least one. On a whim, I decided to check it out.

Long story short, that piece of paper on the bulletin board changed the entire arc of my life. After two interviews, I received an offer of employment. It wasn't at one of the big, prestigious national agencies that might have come calling for my services if I stayed one more year to finish the program. Far from it, in fact. But what a blessing that was, too.

After a quick inventory of my options, I took the short view, and bailed on school. Between getting paid to write and paying a school for the opportunity to practice writing, the former was a much better deal - especially with my Dad's reminder that my return home was a limited proposition. Like all crossroads, the choices we make influence everything that follows. If I had gone the other way, you're probably not reading this – because I'd have lived a completely different life.

The opportunity on that random bulletin board card became my first full-time job in advertising. More importantly, it put me in the path of people who would end up making a huge difference in what I became – as a professional and as a person. The company that hired me was a small, independent ad agency staffed mostly by young up-and-comers trying to find a foothold in the industry. Among them were several people I still count among my best friends to this day. Better yet, less than a year after I started there, we hired a young, talented writer named Carie, who would eventually become my amazing wife.

That first job also launched a series of events that would form my career path up to the present day. I'm sure advertising is like most other industries, where WHAT you know often pales in comparison to WHO you know. As I think back on all the professional jobs I've had, only two of them did I land from a cold, unsolicited recruitment process. In every other instance, I followed a lead from a former colleague to a new company and exponentially expanded my network.

In all cases, I certainly appreciated the kindness of those colleagues who referred me to new opportunities. A couple of times, I've had the chance to repay that kindness and literally Appreciate a situation by growing it in value for myself and others. For instance, that second job introduced me to a couple of creative partners who would become lifelong friends and essentially like family. One of them lives quite far from his own family and thus spends nearly every Christmas with ours. Another became a favorite work partner whose path diverged from mine after we each left the company where we met. But when my new employer needed to fill a position for which she was perfect, I referred her. She was hired, and after a hiatus of several years, we picked up right where we left off, collaborating like we had never missed a day. There, she would meet the man who would one day become her husband. A few years later, they, together with another man we all worked with at this same company, would form an agency of their own. That company, which wouldn't exist without those previous events, would ultimately provide an opportunity that would change my life. More on that just a little bit later.

Small events form chains that link people together in amazing ways. These chains create life narratives that allow each of us to grow and truly appreciate the things that spring from the relationships we develop. One of the great joys of life is when you realize that you have found one of "your people," adding to your family or tribe of folks that you know will be with you in one way or another for the rest of your journey. Recognizing and even growing the value of those significant relationships might seem easy. But appreciating some of the smaller things that happen along the way can be more difficult.

The Best Bad Advice Ever

One of the more confusing experiences I've had came in the form of the single strangest advice I've ever received in a professional context. At the time, I was well into my career, with the same company for several years, and beginning to have a mini-crisis of professional identity. I had been a good performer in my role, doing award- and business-winning work, and often got good feedback from clients and colleagues. But I hadn't really climbed the ladder.

Around that time, I had an annual review with my boss – a woman I loved working for, who shot straight and usually told me what I needed to hear, even if it didn't sound like it at the time. I had been in serious "striver" mode for the six months or so leading up to this review. I had started asking for bigger assignments, stepping up to take the lead where I could, volunteering to travel for presentations, making recommendations about things I thought the company could do better, etc. I figured I was entering a spot where a promotion made sense, both for the company and me, and I was trying to lean into that opportunity.

That review started the way most of them had in the past. I was "good at my job." I was "a valuable member of the team." People enjoyed working with me, and in general, I made the company better with my efforts. All of that sounded good. I was optimistic (which, remember, is not my default). Then, she said the two sentences that I will never forget. The summation of that review, following six months of me actively striving for success, was, "You shouldn't try so hard. You shouldn't care so much."

What? No, seriously – what the hell? Why would you EVER tell any employee, of any company, in any industry, that? I assure you that at the time, not only did I NOT appreciate that; I didn't even understand it. Strangely though, over the next several years, I would find a way to do both.

Right off the bat, you're probably thinking, *"so, you quit, right?"* If your employer told you to stop trying, or even caring, surely, that's not a company worth working for, is it? It turns out, the answer, at least for a while, was "maybe." It did invite some soul-searching, though, which ultimately led to some pretty important realizations about what I was "doing for a LIVING."

On the heels of receiving this truly counterintuitive career advice, I have to say I was confused. Like I said, I had been working in high gear for the previous six months. Had no one noticed? And what would it look like if I *did* stop trying so hard? I decided to find out. It wasn't like I immediately flipped a switch and became a different person overnight. But I did at least plan to test her theory.

Over the next six months, I made a conscious effort to dial it down. I still put 100% effort into my actual work. I still tried hard to come up with great ideas and solid writing to support them. I still tried just as hard to make sure our clients understood and bought those ideas – that was, after all, my job. What I started doing *less* was trying to fix some of the "broken" things I saw about the company itself.

I discovered I was spending significant time and energy being mad, frustrated, and stressed by things that either didn't truly matter or which I didn't have the power to affect. In either case, whether it's what my boss meant or not, she was actually right - sort of. It turned out, "don't try so hard" and even "don't care so much" was excellent advice *when it came to certain things*.

Over those next six months, I became a different employee. I still invested in my work and my team's success, but I became much more disengaged from the company's culture as a whole. What I found at the end of those six months was both terrifying and oddly healthy. It hardly mattered.

In terms of how well I did my job and whether anyone noticed or rewarded me for it or not – it made NO difference at all. That's not to say my work didn't get results. It did. Unfortunately, my company seemed ambivalent about the energy I was investing in getting them and even less interested in appreciating that investment.

What Matters Most

So, here's the crazy part. I stayed with that company for a total of 14 years as a full-time employee. I watched from a disconnected distance as the organization devolved into something I hardly recognized. I watched as nearly everyone I knew, respected, and enjoyed left – some by choice, others by layoffs and corporate restructuring.

Deep down, and long before it all fell apart, I knew this was not a place I was going to grow in leaps in bounds. There wouldn't be frequent promotions or raises, but I also seemed immune to many of the constant changes and staff reductions. So, I stayed.

To most people, that probably makes no sense, but I had my reasons, some of which were better than others. The bottom line: I traded mobility for stability. I stayed where I was comfortable, even though it might have been in my best interest to move on and find something more fulfilling.

I guess the crucial question then is *"what fulfills you?"* or more pointedly, *"what matters most?"*

For me, that line was always a little blurry, even from the very beginning of my tenure at the company. Like most of my career moves, I landed there through a personal connection. Before joining them, I was working as a freelance writer. We had a one-year-old son, and when Carie became pregnant again, she rightly suggested that something more stable than contract work was probably necessary.

So, when this company approached me with an offer to join their staff, it was a blessing we welcomed. The only problem was, they and I were a bit apart on compensation. As a compromise, they suggested I work four days a week for the salary they wanted to pay. Stability being the priority, I accepted. I knew that situation would be different, but I had no idea at the time it would be life-changing.

Prior to that, my context for work-life balance was similar to that of most people who work in corporate America. Monday-Friday was for work, and (if you managed to meet all your deadlines in that timeframe), Saturday and Sunday were for home and family. Something remarkable happened, though, when I started working four days a week. Suddenly, I had an entire day mostly to myself that wasn't scheduled or *owned* by someone else.

What I got in that offer was a gift, a gift of time – the one thing all of us want more of, but which none of us can create. Suddenly, I had eight free hours each week that most people didn't have. That's something worth Appreciating. But I didn't know exactly how yet.

Of course, I intended to fill that extra time with other work to complement the reduced salary I had accepted in return for the flexibility. Sometimes that happened, but honestly, sometimes Monday would roll around, and there were no projects on tap. So, I found myself with extra time, and more importantly, a choice about how to spend it.

Now, I would be lying if I told you I always made the best, smartest decisions with that freedom. Sometimes I allowed the demons of laziness to whisper in my ear and found myself doing very little of value during that time – until I expanded my definition of what I found "valuable." In the absence of work projects, I began to fill that time with other things that mattered.

Our preschool-aged boys were still in daycare at this point. On Mondays, they would always go, but those days became shorter.

Routinely, I'd be able to take them a little later or pick them up a little earlier. Instead of more time in the care of strangers, they were getting more quality time with me. I didn't recognize the full value of that at the time, but that bonus time with our kids – particularly during their formative toddler years – that's a blessing I wouldn't trade for twice the money I might have made "trying harder."

Spending, or I should say investing, extra time with my children is just one of the ways a non-traditional work schedule was legitimately life-changing for me. It also informed my relationship dynamic with Carie.

Go back to my original construct of work-life balance. Far too many people are stuck – either out of necessity or desire – running the traditional "rat race." The weekdays are jam-packed with work and other responsibilities. By the time we get to the weekend, the time when we're supposed to unplug and unwind – if only just to prepare ourselves to start sprinting full-speed again on Monday – we can't. There's grocery shopping, dry cleaning, house cleaning, laundry, yard work, and more – and that doesn't even scratch the surface if you have kids and include their activities in the mix. Honestly, I don't know how ANY of us find the time to get to everything we're supposed to. The answer is that we probably DON'T, which means we make choices, and priorities, and sacrifices.

Many would say the man is supposed to be the provider and protector of his family. But what does that really mean? Traditionally, it meant men were the primary breadwinners, performing work that provides for their family's survival, safety, comfort, and livelihood. Full disclosure – I'm not that, not exactly. Or am I? I guess it depends on what you consider counting as contributions to those goals.

Here's where, once again, I get to sing the praises of my incredible wife. For a very brief time in our relationship, I was technically the breadwinner. But I could have told you long ago that probably wouldn't last. You see, Carie is one of the most dedicated and hard-working people I know – she reminds me of both of my parents in that regard. Over the course of our decades together, I've described her as "hard-working" on countless occasions. It's always been a compliment, but it's only recently that I think I've realized that I've probably sold her a little short. What I really mean to say is that Carie is one of the greatest Appreciators I know. That might sound vague, but it's pretty simple. Essentially, *whatever* Carie is given (a marriage, children, a career, volunteer opportunities, friendships), Carie invests in it with her whole self and invariably increases its value. Appreciation; everywhere, constantly. This investment mode is hard-wired within her. It's who she is. That's why, after 20+ years of hard work and investment, in herself and others, all at the same company, Carie now finds herself rightfully in the senior leadership for a global company directing teams doing important work with impressive budgets and impact. No one who knows Carie even a little bit is surprised by this outcome.

So, what does all that have to do with my career? Plenty. For starters, everything I just described about Carie is a gift to me. Her tenacity, endless patience, and energy are inspirational, even if I don't have them in equal measure. Her selflessness is humbling and brings with it a realization. Even though her passion *is* hardwired, meaning she'd probably be kicking just as much butt professionally if our boys and I weren't part of her reality, we *are* part of her life. We're the ones she chooses to bless, with her presence, her love, her talents, and the fruits of her labor. That alone is as big a gift as any person could hope to receive. And it has plenty of benefits. For example, through her talents and dedication, Carie has effectively created both stability and flexibility. Stability in her own career because she has Appreciated every opportunity she's been given and has become so trusted and valued within her company. And an uncommon degree of flexibility for me to operate dually as a freelance writer and stay-at-home parent.

Again, it comes down to choices and priorities. We could have made different decisions, and we would probably have more money, but I doubt seriously if we would be any "richer" than we already are. There isn't a single day that goes by that I don't recognize the value of what Carie's efforts help create for our family.

The question then becomes: "What can I give in return?" or better yet, "How can I Appreciate that?"

It comes right back to "time." As our career paths continue, I often find myself with a surplus of it, while Carie increasingly struggles to find enough time each day just to keep up with the growing demands of her ever-growing role.

You know the old saying, "time is money." It's true in more than one sense. Most people would agree you can spend time making money, but no amount of money can buy you more time. I'd say that's not necessarily true. In forgoing a portion of a salary, I was doing precisely that – "buying time" in exchange for more time away from work. Again, the question is: how do you Appreciate that?

For one thing, I can continue to think differently about the value of time. Most days, I consider "creating time and space" for Carie as a part of my "job description." If she's spending her time winning bread and providing for our family, what can I do to honor and complement that? Creating time and space for her to focus on being as awesome as she is at work without having to worry about sixteen other things on some phantom "to-do" list at home is a decent start.

That balancing act may look different day to day, but it always comes from the same place. Recognizing the immense value of how she is spending her time makes me want to return that gift in the form of as much extra time I can create for her. The net result is more time for us to enjoy each other and our family. As I said, it's non-traditional, but most of the time, it works. I might have pumped the brakes on my own ride a little, but the truth is, stepping back probably helped us move forward and created a net gain for our family.

So, you've also heard the phrase, "if it's not broke, don't fix it," right? Well, what happens when something that's been working for years finally breaks?

***

After 14 years, I finally left the company that wanted me to "not try so hard and not care so much." My tenure there was full of changes and transitions, but the last six months were particularly tumultuous. It started with another round of layoffs. This time, they were extreme.

Nearly half our creative staff was terminated, including many of the people I cared about and enjoyed working with the most. Most shocking to me, that boss who gave me the craziest advice ever was let go too. You might think I'd have felt some relief from that, but quite the opposite was true. Even if her methods were non-traditional, in many ways, she was a really good boss. She trusted me, and others, implicitly to follow our instincts and do our jobs. She allowed us freedom both creatively and as people. She gave credit where credit was due, and she held us accountable when we made mistakes. She listened when we had issues, even if she didn't have the power to solve them. And she defended our team fiercely, falling on the sword when necessary. All of those are qualities I admire in people and respect in leaders. And it lends credence to the adage, *"people don't quit their jobs, they quit their bosses."* In the years we spent working together, I learned quite a lot from her, even if a lot of it wouldn't necessarily fall in the category of business knowledge or professional development.

Instead, I'd say most of the best lessons I took from that relationship were about treating people and circumstances correctly. Specifically, I learned the importance of giving things, people, and situations exactly (and only) the investment they deserve. Not everything, or everyone, in your life, deserves 100% of your time, energy, or even respect. I don't mean that dismissively. Nor am I suggesting some things or people are inferior to others. But I will say that I have lived with considerably less stress on the whole since I stopped wasting as much energy on things that don't "appreciate" my investment in them. I'm not sure that's exactly what she meant, but it's a pretty good application of "not caring so much."

So, in some ways, maybe this boss did prepare me for life without her. That premise was about to be tested in a way I never saw coming.

It started with me being summoned to the company's corporate offices in New York for a creative team meeting. It wasn't until I called the manager of that office – inquiring about coordinating flights with my coworkers from Atlanta – that I learned I was the ONLY person from my office invited to this meeting. Shortly after that, I learned that my boss and most of my long-time friends and creative teammates were laid off. I had to fly to New York to meet my new boss, who seemed nice but was someone I didn't know well at all. I was also going to meet the Global Creative Director to hear his vision for how the other survivors and I were supposed to move forward – another "opportunity" I didn't necessarily appreciate.

I spent most of that trip in New York in a bit of a daze. The truth is, I almost didn't get on the plane at all. I had very serious conversations with Carie about quitting then and there. Some of that desire was out of loyalty to the many talented people whose absences I was sure were going to weaken the remaining company. And partly, I was in dread fear of the unknown future before me. In the end, I decided to at least meet the new team and hear the new guy out. Maybe I'd instantly like him and be reassured that the New World Order was going to be palatable, or even somehow a hidden blessing. So, I went.

I'd be lying if I said any of those best-case scenarios played out over those two days in New York. I did get a chance to reconnect with a couple of old colleagues from other offices who also survived. And everyone else I met for the first time was nice enough, but the mood was anything but festive. I distinctly remember sitting in the conference room, half-listening to our new Director talk about strategic visions and thinking, *"none of this even matters now; I'm not staying."* I called Carie that first night from the hotel. She again talked me off the ledge of quitting the next morning. It wasn't so much that she changed my mind and talked me into buying in. It was something far more valuable. That was the beginning of an ongoing conversation we would have for a while about figuring out the "right way to quit a job." Oddly, it was also the beginning of the journey that included the biggest hidden blessings in all this seeming chaos.

Outside of losing my job outright, that chaos began with nearly as much change to the work life I was used to as possible. For several years prior, I had been working exclusively from home, which I really enjoy. Now, it seemed the company had a new vision, one that would require me to commute to a new office they were going to open in Atlanta. At first, that idea made very little sense. Why did they need a new office for two people in Atlanta? Because the rest of the plan was that my colleague and I would be hiring and managing a new (younger, and presumably less expensive) team. So, suddenly, I went from working with a group of long-trusted colleagues, remotely from home, where I was self-directed, highly efficient, and in control of my own time and environment, to the polar opposite of all that. Nope. I didn't appreciate that a bit.

I remember with painful clarity the first day I saw the new space in which we would be working. My colleague – a woman I'd known for a little while and genuinely liked and respected – met me there, and our reactions couldn't have been more different. She lived in town, less than a mile from the new office space. I commuted from the suburbs, a trip that took more than an hour in

Atlanta traffic. Upon my arrival, my partner, also a cynic by nature but slightly more optimistic, looked at me and said, "this isn't so bad." I was almost in tears of frustration. The "this" she referred to was a glass box, approximately the size of a standard prison cell. Our company had jumped in on the co-working space craze, and our new "office" was one of a whole row of such cells jammed into a floor of a high-rise building in midtown Atlanta. Glass box after glass box; human terrariums for the hip, upstart working class. After "Hello," I'm pretty sure the second thing my friend heard me say that morning was, "I hate everything about this." Not a momentous start to our new adventure.

The first month of that new arrangement was mostly about figuring out the transition. We had to maintain productivity and client demands while changing everything else about how (and with whom) we worked. I still cared about doing the best creative work I could. And as a pleasant surprise, the challenge we'd both inherited seemed to strengthen the bond I already had with my colleague. For better or worse, we were in the fight together and at least had each other for collaboration and commiseration.

Then we began the process of seeking new team members to join us. For starters, we would each add one new employee under our direction. Those additions would help with the growing workload. But they would also double the occupancy of our little glass box. The commute, thin walls, loud neighbors, and other aspects of this environment were already affecting my productivity and morale. I couldn't imagine adding two more bodies and voices to that mix could be a positive. I was still waiting for the blessing in disguise.

My dissatisfaction was growing. Sensing a change was inevitable, I had begun to look in earnest for new opportunities. That search was a two-pronged strategy, and the results of each couldn't have been more different. I hit the online employment websites and job postings from various local companies. The sound of crickets was deafening as every cold resume I sent disappeared into a black hole, many without even a response. The other path, my freelance network, was a totally different experience.

After 20+ years working in one industry, in one city, my local professional network was solid. I started reaching out to people I had worked with previously to see what opportunities were out there. Phone calls and emails led to lunches or meetings over drinks with several old associates. All of these were fruitful to some degree. Most encouragingly, to a person, everyone I met with expressed enthusiasm for collaborating again. Several of them came through with projects I could work on immediately, which was a great way for both sides to test the waters of working together.

I've never been a fan of burning bridges and have tried hard never to do it professionally. The satisfaction of telling someone off when you leave a job might be a momentary adrenaline rush or a salve for hurt feelings, but it's always short-lived. Most local industries are small worlds. You see the same people over and over, and bad experiences can be tough to outlive. So, it was gratifying to know that my personal and professional reputation seemed in good standing and that people were willing to work with me.

As I continued to mine my network, the projects kept coming. Those would help create a financial cushion to soften my landing when the time came to jump ship from my job. Except, I still had that job. And by now, I was working the equivalent of another one, or more, in freelance gigs. That's a good problem to have, but also a source of stress. I was burning the candle at both ends, but it was creating light at the end of the tunnel, and just in time.

Even though some of the extra stress I was feeling was "good," in total, the strain was starting to affect my physical and mental health. I knew as the number of things I was trying to juggle increased, the time, attention, and quality I could offer each of them was starting to suffer. My family was seeing less of me. The team I was still a part of at my full-time job was not getting my best work or leadership. I started to see some of the other things in my world (friends, church, coaching, etc.) as obligations I "had to make time for," rather than things I looked forward to with joy. Essentially, there was NOTHING in my world that was getting the 100% of me it deserved. Then, something life-changing happened.

A New Lifeline from the Old Crew

Remember those friends I told you about earlier – the ones who got married after meeting at the company I recruited her to join? Well, by now, they had started a small agency of their own. So, of course, they were among the folks I reached out to as I started planning to make a change. When I called to see if there was anything they might need help with, they invited me to lunch to talk. Of course, I was excited and interested but also determined not to get ahead of myself. I hoped there might be some small projects in the offing, which would be helpful and appreciated. But it could also end up being a casual reconnect with friends I hadn't seen in a while. It *was* that, but so much more.

Somewhere near the middle of lunch, after we'd caught up on family life, kids, and a few former clients and coworkers, my friend turned to me and asked, "So, what are you looking for?" I don't know if he meant to be so pointed with his question, but it was perfect, both in its phrasing and the opportunity it provided for a response. And by that, I don't even mean that it was a "softball" question; more the opposite. It was so direct that it caught me off guard. My brain flew into overdrive, trying to decide between the MANY possible ways I could answer that question. What DID I want?

Years later, I'm still incredibly grateful for that question. Fueled by the frustration of my current situation and encouraged by the "safety" of being among friends, I answered with clarity and honesty. I told them, "All I really want is to be able to do fun, interesting, challenging work with people I trust and like." Simple enough, and a thoroughly genuine answer. It's probably what most people would "want" if they got to pick their dream scenario off a menu. But, try putting that wish out into the universe – or in cover letters on applications and see what comes back. Cue those crickets again.

It was the perfect time for God to remind me He'd been involved in the process all along.

My friends could have laughed at my answer or told me: "Yeah, isn't that what EVERYONE wants?" Instead, they had their own story to tell. After several years in business, their small agency was hitting a growth spurt. At the same time I was looking for a new opportunity, they found they had more work than they could handle on their own. They had relationships with several other freelance writers in town, but what they really needed was someone to serve in a more consistent capacity, someone looking for "almost" a full-time job. Hmm.

I had run the numbers, and I knew that "almost" a full-time job's worth of freelance assignments was the security net I needed to be able to quit my current job. And, conversations I'd had with other former colleagues led me to believe I could bridge the rest of the time and salary gap.

From the time I learned of the massive layoffs that took most of my favorite teammates away, I'd been praying for literal deliverance from a situation I just couldn't "appreciate" anymore. And I mean that in every sense of the word. I was so disillusioned; I could no longer even see, let alone try to increase its value. It took several months for all the pieces to fall into place, but somehow, in this one casual lunch conversation with my friends, I seemed to be staring the answer to that prayer squarely in the face.

For months, I had been walking through a journey of change. My focus was on finding a new job. But I also worried about finding the "right way" to leave a company I had been part of for more than a decade. That was a complicated equation. I needed to replace the frustrations and stress I felt with a new situation. I needed to ensure some financial stability. AND I needed not to burn the longest bridge I had built thus far in my career. It should have been easy enough to accept my friends' offer and bail on my current employer, but I was oddly conflicted.

Here was the problem. Remember those people my partner and I had to hire when we planted the new office? It turns out they were great, and not just professionally. Like my partner, the people we hired were genuinely decent humans who were engaging, easy to work with, and fun. That's not a problem at all – but leaving them, especially after only five months of training, might be. Not for me, of course; I'd be on to greener pastures, and they'd be the ones left to deal with all the things I didn't appreciate. There's the problem.

Once I knew I was leaving, I developed a sense of guilt over leaving my partner in a lurch. She didn't love our situation any more than I did, and here I was bailing on her. Same for the new hires. They'd joined a new company, and now one of the people who invited them to be part of this small team was up and leaving after just a few months. It would be hard to blame them if they were cynical about stability or the future.

Now I was beginning to consider the effect my actions were about to have on others. I was making a "selfish" decision, one that was going to make their lives more difficult. I was sure they weren't going to appreciate that. As I considered this, I had a realization. I had no emotional connection to the company itself, but I was still very much invested in some of the people. In particular, I had an epiphany about something I certainly didn't expect when all of these changes began.

Sometimes Quitters Do Win

One of the people we hired was a junior writer who would work directly under my supervision. The successful candidate was young and not that far removed from having graduated college. She had some prior professional writing experience, but not in our industry. She interviewed well and showed plenty of knowledge and promise, but she was also a blank slate when it came to working in an advertising agency. It would be my job to teach her everything I could – about our company and the industry, including agency dynamics, client relationships, etc. And that's in addition to teaching her the actual job duties of being a writer. For the first time in a long time, I would be responsible for someone other than myself professionally. My job now included ensuring the quality of someone else's work, and more importantly, trying to help them learn and grow.

Now, recall my state of mind during this whole process. I was partially checked-out mentally, disgruntled with a corporate culture that had recently fired many of my friends, and not very happy at all about losing my work-from-home scenario in favor of a commute and supervisory responsibilities. If you were going to build the World's Worst Boss in a lab, that would be an excellent starter kit. And for most new employees, those conditions – even if you were wholly unaware of them coming in – would not be a recipe for success. Luckily for everyone involved, especially me, the perfect person for the job showed up.

As I said, our new writer was young and a little green, but she was also curious and humble. I'd quickly discover she also possessed exceptional attention to detail, the ability to ask smart questions and think creatively, and a genuine desire to contribute. In stark contrast, and perhaps with a smirk of irony, it was as if God sent the World's Worst Boss a gift in the form of the World's Best Employee. Here comes the epiphany.

Part of my dread for my new managerial responsibility – aside from my lack of enthusiasm for my own job – was the realization that I didn't feel at all prepared to be anyone's boss, leader, or mentor.

I mentioned my former boss earlier – the one who told me to stop trying so hard. Here, I feel the need to reiterate that she *was* a good boss. In a lot of ways, I wouldn't have hardly changed any of it. One thing I did realize, though, is that across my entire career, there was a constant. I have had a lot of bosses, but I have never had a true MENTOR – someone who took a particular interest in helping me develop as an individual, as well as an employee. I don't think I ever thought about that until it was my turn to lead someone else. In performance reviews, regardless of company or boss, I always scored high for being self-directed, productive, and effective. Perhaps I was seen as someone who didn't *need* oversight or mentorship. Although I see now that ALL of us can benefit from the guiding hand of someone who has already been where we are and is interested in maximizing our success.

Back to the World's Best Employee. In this person, I saw many of the same strengths in her that others had suggested of me. Better still, she seemed to have all those positive attributes without the baggage of the negative ones that weigh me down – cynicism, sarcasm, selective laziness, etc. In this person, I had the ideal mentee. And on some other level, I was being given an even more generous gift – an opportunity to try to be the kind of boss I never had myself. I mean that in a different way than it probably sounds. I realize that my former bosses likely had a ton of managerial duties that were far more pressing than micromanaging every person on their staff – especially ones who seemed to do just fine on their own. What I mean is that I was in a unique position at that point.

I knew from almost the very beginning of this hire's tenure; I wouldn't be there with her for the long haul. It didn't take her long to prove her worth; she *was* the World's Best Employee after all. But it was still surprising how quickly I became invested in wanting her to succeed. Because I knew I was leaving, I was no longer focused on my own survival or success. That meant I had the unique luxury of making HER success my primary focus for most of the five short months we had together.

Something happens to us when our energy is focused on others before, or instead of, ourselves. In my personal experience, wherever I have discovered that dynamic – whether in the role of parent, coach, mentor, spouse, or friend – my capacity for Appreciation has been vastly magnified.

So, in numerous ways, I had found something new to Appreciate about a decade-plus long career stop that had long since lost its shine. But that's not even the end of the story.

Remember how I was struggling with figuring out the "right way" to quit my job? Well, after that fateful lunch date with my friends (and my soon-to-be new employers), I came home and told Carie I thought I had found my parachute. We agreed the time had finally arrived for me to call my boss in New York and tender my resignation. I had a new gig lined up, but I was still nervous about making that call. I had been there so long, and I knew that my leaving was going to come as a surprise. And I genuinely had no interest in making anyone's life more difficult. So, even though there was some joy in getting closure on a situation that had been causing me stress for a long time, I definitely had mixed emotions.

Part of the reason I was so nervous was that I fully expected my boss to be angry. I was prepared for her to tell me that I didn't even need to work out a notice and could leave immediately. She didn't say any of that. My boss listened as I explained how I could no longer maintain the stress and frustration I felt. NOBODY was getting my best in this situation. I needed to change my life, and that meant me leaving the company. Her response was almost as shocking as my former boss' advice to "not try so hard." What she told me was, "Don't just leave. How much of you can we keep?"

Wait. What? I just quit my job of 14 years to join a company that was offering to fill about 70% of my current time and salary. My boss could have slammed the door on me outright, then and there. Instead, their response was basically: *"Okay. We understand. But we still think you can be valuable here in a limited capacity, so we'll still take as much of you as we can get."* Wow. I didn't expect or know how to respond to that. My boss and I talked for a while longer, and I agreed to take the weekend to put together an exit plan and what a part-time relationship might look like moving forward. I was in tears when I hung up the phone. I was relieved that something I was dreading was finally over. But that was only part of it. The empathy my boss had shown in understanding my situation was unexpected. The appreciation she showed for my value to the company, including the mentoring I had done thus far with our new junior writer – who had already grown in leaps and bounds – was genuinely overwhelming. My boss accepted my resignation out of respect for my needs. She also asked me to stay involved with the company, and our new writers, out of respect for my ability. That's incredibly gratifying. It's also about as "right" of an outcome as one can expect from quitting a job.

Conversely, imagine what would have happened had I given in to my desire to quit before even going to New York, or while I was there, or any of the other times I considered it. If I had left when I wanted to, I would have robbed myself of numerous opportunities. I wouldn't have seen my working relationship with my then-partner become hardened by adversity and bloom into a genuine friendship. I wouldn't have met several new colleagues who have also become friends. I wouldn't have a chance to appreciate the World's Best Employee, with whom I still speak frequently and to whom I have offered to remain available as a mentor for as long as I can be of service to her.

Instead, by being patient and trusting that something better was coming, even if I couldn't even see it yet, I was the beneficiary of so many gifts.

I learned that before I could be properly "released" from the situation I no longer wanted to be in, I needed to be reminded of how much I had to Appreciate about it. Those lessons of patience, appreciation, and gratitude have significantly influenced how I approach and value my current job. They've also taught me how to better Appreciate the balance between "what I do" and "who I am."

Now, when someone asks me, *"what do you do for a living?"* I think the best answer might be: "I live." By this, I mean there is an intentional desire to be present, to actually LIVE instead of just working. Of course, work is a necessary and good part of a healthy life. But focusing on appreciating our opportunities and performing our jobs with balance and a sense of thanksgiving can change everything about how we view and approach work itself.

• What do YOU do (for a living)?

• Has your vision of the role your job plays in your overall identity evolved? How so?

• How much different would your approach or perspective on an upcoming challenge be if you knew beforehand you have everything you needed to succeed?

• Who is the best boss you have ever had? What is it about that person you appreciate most? Have you ever told them?

• When have you had to exercise extreme patience in a situation you knew wasn't right, but whose alternative had not yet revealed itself? Were you successful (because or despite that decision)?

Wisdom to Appreciate:

Philippians 4:6 - "Do not be anxious or worried about anything, but in everything [every circumstance and situation] by prayer and petition with thanksgiving, continue to make your [specific] requests known to God."

Hebrews 11:6 - "God is a rewarder of them who seek Him."

Chapter 5:
The Search for a Church

To say that my wife Carie and I had different spiritual upbringings is an understatement. She was raised in the Baptist tradition in places like Alabama, California, and Texas. When I was six years old, my parents moved us from Ohio to Georgia, where we joined a non-denominational Christian church, which I would attend until moving to South Carolina for college.

From the ages of 6-18, I experienced a variety of other churches and religious groups. I attended Catholic services with my grandparents. I made pilgrimages to lauded cathedrals like Martin Luther King Jr.'s Ebenezer Baptist for Wednesday worship services. I visited the Methodist and Episcopal congregations of my friends and classmates. I took Comparative Religion courses in college, gaining knowledge and perspective on faiths including Judaism, Islam, Buddhism, and more. I found something that made at least a little bit of sense in all those experiences – and maybe nothing that made complete sense. In general, I would say I was open to considering most of it.

Then something happened that made NO sense at all. If you're reading this book sequentially, you already know that thing was the death of my sister, Kim. On the off chance you're skipping around, I'll reiterate the crux for context. On April 15th, 1993, when my sister died from cancer at the young age of 23, whatever faith I had in God up to that point went with her. I had prayed hard, earnestly, and desperately for God to spare Kim's life, and I was sure I had seen Him flatly disregard those prayers. I didn't appreciate that. At the age of 21, I walked away for God. I'm not sure I ever intended to come back.

Again, I am reminded of Jeremiah 29:11. *"For I know the plans I have for you, declares the Lord, plans for welfare and not for evil, to give you a future and a hope."*

In this instance, I definitely didn't see any grand Master Plan in what God was showing me in real time. As so often seems the case, I was only seeing a fraction of the big picture. But there was plenty more happening beyond my view. My cynical eyes saw with clarity what I was sure God had *taken* from me. But I had no vision for what He was going to *give* me.

In His infinite wisdom, God sent me one of His most patient daughters as a guide, as a partner, and as an example of His own patience as He waited for me to return. I met Carie about five years after my sister died; five years during which I only set foot in a church for other peoples' weddings or funerals, and during which I virtually had no relationship with God at all. I was actively angry and neither capable nor desirous of seeing anything to Appreciate.

Over the next several years, Carie and I would build a relationship – first as professional colleagues, then as friends, and eventually starting a romance destined for matrimony. Those early years of our relationship were not without struggle or disagreement, though, and the subjects of church and God were often involved. The longer our relationship went on, the more frequent these conversations became, and the clearer I became that my divorce from God was not an issue likely to be left alone.

As I've said, Carie is remarkably patient – a fact I credit hugely for the resilience of our 20+ year relationship. But all things have their limits. There are a lot of Sundays over the course of five or six years. As more of those would pass without us attending church, Carie's longing to feed her own spiritual hunger, and her lament at not doing so, continued to grow. And so, we would continue to talk.

We started to have a conversation about going to church. I was minimally open to the idea, but mostly because I knew it was important to her, not because it was something I wanted to do. In the beginning, those conversations didn't go far without breaking down – and the sticking point was clear. How were we ever going to find a church that was pleasing, or even palatable, to both of us?

We were both raised in the Christian church, but the distance on that spectrum was significant. Her point of reference was Biblically traditional. In contrast, I was used to more modern applications of those teachings that focused on showing us simply how to "live the right way" and be good people.

Over the years, we visited numerous churches – most notably those of our parents, whenever our travels to their homes included a Sunday morning. Carie's parents attended Baptist services, and mine had transitioned toward the Presbyterian denomination. So, we were already familiar with both of those perspectives as our search began. Whether it was the context of my upbringing or a lingering frustration with God in general, I didn't find any real connection to, or comfort from, those services. Sermons questioning the purity of my soul, and the weighty choice between salvation and eternal damnation, were not things I can honestly say I was in a place to be able to appreciate. These were not the churches where I was likely to find a spiritual home.

We also explored the opposite end of the Christian spectrum. The non-denominational church where I grew up still had a congregation in Atlanta. Carie and I decided to pay a visit. I knew this place had changed in the decades since I was last there, but it was almost unrecognizable for the church of my childhood. As much as I wanted it to be the welcoming, comforting place I had tucked away in my memory, it was now something completely different. It had changed, and so had I. That wasn't going to be it either.

As the months would pass, we'd occasionally visit other churches near us, but nothing seemed to fit. We were living in a Goldilocks paradox. Every church was either "too hard" or "too soft." I would have been fine with giving up our search altogether, declaring, *"Hey, we tried. There's just no solution that's going to make everyone happy."* There's my cynical mind again, attacking and allowing defeat as an option. Did I mention that my wife is both awesome and not at all wired this way?

It may have been that our plans to start a family ratcheted up her need to solve the challenge of finding a church to call home. Just as likely, it was a matter of faith. Hers is strong, and when problems arise that she can't see a solution to, she prays.

When God Comes Knocking

By this time, Carie had finished graduate school, and we were expecting our second child. We had just settled into a lovely new abode but still hadn't found a spiritual home. Then, God made a literal house call.

To fully appreciate what happened next, it's helpful to make an accounting of where my spiritual mind was at the time. We were doing relatively well, and my blessings were many. But cynicism and grudges are resilient. I had a wonderful wife, a nice home, professional opportunities, a toddler, and another child on the way. But I still wasn't particularly interested in praising God for those things. I was still actively mad at him – holding onto the pain of the few prayers I thought He *hadn't* answered, instead of seeing the many He had.

In terms of finding a church, I had built a concrete mental barrier. We'd tried lots of places, and none of them were checking the boxes of the narrow criteria I was going to deem acceptable. When we would visit those churches, I couldn't always explain it, but I never felt right or comfortable. Almost without exception, those experiences felt heavy and not particularly positive.

Whether in truth or perception, my takeaways usually included a sense of judgment or even condemnation and not much encouragement. Most of those church experiences felt very "old school" in nature. There were the traditional hymns, hundreds of years old, that never really stirred my soul. Then, traditional sermons which often felt cold, critical, or unrelatable. And finally, a traditional passing of the plate that felt obligatory or even forced, as though I was being charged admission for a show I wasn't particularly enjoying. None of that was working for me or growing my desire to develop a relationship with God. The more of "God's people" I met, the more I felt like I probably just wasn't meant to be one of them. And if the price of membership was changing who I knew I was to conform to those traditions that felt awkward and inauthentic, I wasn't interested.

Those were the bricks in the wall I had built. *"These religious traditions aren't accessible. I love music, but this music doesn't connect with me at all. This is not who I am. God must not love who I am. If He truly wants a relationship with me, surely He can figure out a way to talk to me that at least makes sense."* In short, God wasn't making it easy for me, and well, I didn't appreciate it.

So, that's where I was: stuck, in mind and spirit. Then, like every other day before that, I went to check the mail. Among the bills and junk mail was a simple 4x6" postcard with God's response to my wall of objections. Fifteen years later, I still have it. It said:

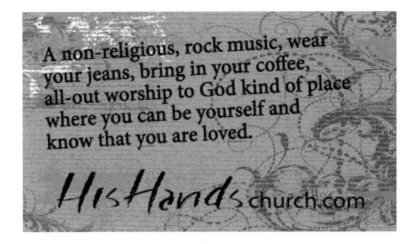

A non-religious, rock music, wear your jeans, bring in your coffee, all-out worship to God kind of place where you can be yourself and know that you are loved.

HisHands church.com

Seriously? It was as if God had been sitting across a table from me, patiently taking notes on what I was looking for, and then carefully crafting a reply. What's more, it was a response I couldn't even argue. On that level alone, I had to appreciate it.

As an advertising writer, I spend hours every day arranging words to convince audiences of a particular message, or to coerce them into specific actions. That doesn't exactly help one become less cynical. But it does make you slightly more attuned to this form of "manipulation" when you encounter it in other places. So, even though I would willingly go along for the ride, it would be dishonest to say I wasn't skeptical that this postcard might be overselling its proposition.

Before receiving this card, I couldn't even imagine finding a church that would satisfy me (let alone be equally desirous to Carie). But, at least on face value, here was an invitation to a place that seemed to be tailor-made to the (admittedly narrow) specifications I had placed on God. When something like that is staring you right in the face, the only way to miss it is if you're purposefully trying NOT to see it.

Carie's immediate reaction to that postcard? "Wow, isn't this pretty much everything you would say you wanted?" Great. Now I had seen it, AND I had to ACKNOWLEDGE it too. I guess I could now (small-a) appreciate that such a thing was at least possible.

I can be pretty stubborn, but could I really ignore or turn down an invitation this coincidental, or that divinely inspired? Knowing how important finding a church was to Carie, I also knew we would soon be paying a visit.

The Barrier Between God and Me

A few short days later, we put on our jeans, packed up our coffee, and headed to Sunday services at His Hands Church in Woodstock, GA. The fact that it was a 25-minute drive from our house wasn't even an obstacle. It was oddly reminiscent of my childhood, where our parents drove about 40 minutes each way for church – a ride I never minded, as it took me to one of my favorite places at the time.

If the "traditional" aspects (messages, hymns, attire, etc.) were part of what made me uncomfortable in my visits to other churches, His Hands was disarming from the very start. The building itself was anything but traditional. In fact, it had been a K-Mart in its previous life.

A few friendly, happy people welcomed us and directed us through a large lobby area to what they referred to as "the Big Room" instead of the "Sanctuary." Even in details as small as how they referred to physical parts of their building, His Hands was reinforcing the authenticity of the message they'd sent us in that fateful postcard. I still couldn't find anything to be upset or put off by. We made our way into the Big Room and found a place amongst a few hundred people. There we sat and waited for what came next.

What came next was music, and even more stones in my wall gave way. A few poor efforts in college bands aside, I am no musician. I can't read notes and don't have a tuned ear or voice.

But music has always been a central and powerful force in my life. It speaks to me on an emotional, spiritual level. I've often told Carie, who is a fierce and loyal prayer, that I rarely, if ever, "hear from God" in prayer, but I DO hear from Him and genuinely feel the presence of the Holy Spirit through music.

So, to say that I had high hopes for this "rock music," The Card of Destiny had promised me was an understatement. I knew there were Christian rock bands – but I didn't listen to them, so I didn't know what to expect. I knew from experience that standing in a cavernous sanctuary as a massive pipe organ blared traditional hymns like "Bringing in the Sheaves" over a sleepy flock of parishioners did absolutely nothing for me. I knew from being in places like Ebenezer Baptist, marveling at the sheer force of some of those gospel choir performances, that my soul could stir to the Word of God in music. I just hadn't heard or felt that in a very long time.

The worship band at His Hands more than held up their part of The Card's promise too. Strong, passionate voices, backed by a full band of electric guitars, bass, keyboards, and drums, guided the congregation through a slate of contemporary songs I didn't even know. But they somehow felt relatable and accessible. I don't know that the deepest reaches of my soul were touched on that first day, but my soul was at least open and receptive. That was progress. We had been there for more than thirty minutes, and I still wasn't mad or disappointed. Maybe The Card, and the experience it offered, was a little more authentic than I wanted to admit was possible.

When the music was over, a man in his forties, with salt and pepper hair, dressed in jeans and an untucked colorful dress shirt, took the stage. He introduced himself as Steve and began to share a message that I can't honestly say I recall in any detail. Partly, this is because that encounter happened 15 years before this writing. The larger truth is, I wasn't focused on the specific details of his message. This was more like a first date or an interview. I'd gotten an invitation, which I accepted skeptically. I showed up with tempered expectations. Against those expectations, my first impressions had been surprisingly positive. But, as any good cynic will tell you, there could be something waiting just around the next bend that takes the train entirely off its tracks.

So, more than listening and really digesting the meat of Steve's message, I was experiencing (and probably critiquing) it on a different level. I was sizing it up for content but also tone and intent. Any minute, I was sure we would get to the part about how we're all awful sinners, condemned to an eternity of suffering in Hell, lest we repent. As soon as I heard that, I could dismiss this His Hands as a "nice try" and go right back to being sure there wasn't a church for me.

Except, I didn't get any of that. Instead, I heard a man talk to me about how he didn't always hear God – until he did. And even then, he couldn't be sure he (or God Himself) wasn't crazy. Because what God was telling Steve – a very successful businessman with no previous designs on being a minister – was that he and his wife Susan should take the multiple millions gained from the sale of their very successful technology company and start a church. Apparently, unbeknownst to Steve, God had been telling Susan the exact same thing. After much discussion and prayer, they would both listen and obey.

At first, this church with no building would meet on Sunday mornings in a local Dave and Buster's entertainment complex. Slowly, interest grew, and along with it, a congregation of like-minded souls. Steve and Susan began looking for a building to house this new church. Finally, through a series of divinely guided events, they discovered a vacant K-Mart. In pure obedience to the direction they were both receiving from God, Steve and Susan would re-invest an unbelievable amount of their personal fortune – which they knew to be a blessing from Him in the first place – into purchasing that K-Mart and renovating it into the very non-traditional church we were visiting.

He went on to explain the dynamic of God and man in a way that made more sense to me than anything I'd heard since my childhood. Speaking in simple, modern terms, Steve walked a path of thought that centered on the crucial difference between the two trees in the Garden of Eden – the Tree of Life and the Tree of the Knowledge of Good and Evil. His earnest, easy-going temperament was more akin to a teacher sharing wisdom than a preacher shouting condemnation. The more he talked, the easier he was to listen to, and the further down my guard slipped. And then, after I had already been beautifully disarmed by a friendly environment, some soul-rousing rock worship, and the casual frankness of Steve's presentation, he said something that changed everything.

Steve further explained that ever since man was fatefully tricked into eating from the Tree of the Knowledge of Good and Evil – with the Devil's promise that they would be like God – there was a division between man and God. Centuries passed, with people making an endless string of poor decisions. Worse, we made countless rules and regulations for how one was to live a righteous life. All these rules were essentially "religion," and not at all what God Himself had in mind for us as his children.

Understanding that these human-made, religious ideals were driving us further away from Him, God put a plan in action to change everything. God sent Jesus to us – to live life as a man, as a perfect representation of God's love. And, it was through Jesus, through accepting His teachings, His example, and ultimately His sacrifice, that we would be able to remove all barriers between God and us.

Wait. Say that again. You're telling me there's a path I can take that leads to removing all the barriers between God and me? THAT's the message The Card of Destiny brought me to this renovated K-Mart to hear? I just spent the last 15 years of my life going out of my way to *create* those barriers between myself and

God. That message landed squarely and with some weight. I kind of didn't appreciate that.

And here was the "worst" part. Even though I was more than a little annoyed at having been convicted, it was the kind of conviction I couldn't really be mad about because even if my mind wanted to argue about it, somewhere deeper down, I knew it was true.

When that Sunday service ended, I was not only convicted but also conflicted. On the one hand, I had genuinely enjoyed the morning. At the very least, I was intrigued by what I had experienced. More surprisingly, I was open to experiencing it again. And somehow, there was still the other part of me – the stubborn cynic – who still needed to look at the downside. I actually had a voice in my head saying, *"Well, I can't find anything to NOT like about that. Now, I guess I have to admit I was wrong, and NOW, I guess we'll probably have to talk about actually coming to church regularly. And I honestly, I DON'T APPRECIATE THAT."*

In this instance, "I don't appreciate that" really just translates into "that's not very convenient for me." I'd spent years digging my heels in when it came to not going to church or even having a relationship with God. I had processed Him not answering my specific prayers as Him turning His back on me – and I had been all too happy to respond in kind. Now, it felt like I had something telling me, *"You know, it doesn't have to be like this – if you don't want it to be."*

Don't get me wrong. It wasn't as if I got hit by a bolt of lightning that first Sunday at His Hands and was supernaturally transformed. I still had all that pain and anger, and distrust. But somehow, at least another voice was now allowed to be heard alongside all the cynicism.

The car ride home from that first Sunday service was interesting. It featured a new version of a conversation Carie and I had had many times. After visits to other churches, we usually both knew before even talking about it that what we had just experienced wasn't the magic solution that was going to make everyone happy. This conversation was different. I'm sure one of us turned to the other and asked plainly, "So, what did you think of that?" Both of us may have been hesitant to do so, but for different reasons. For her part, she'd been down this road before – walking out of a service she probably thought of as pretty reasonable, only to see that I found it completely unacceptable. For me, this was something different and new. I'd actually found His Hands to be a perfectly acceptable option that didn't push any of my buttons the wrong way. That being the case, I almost expected her to have some objections, just because I was predisposed to believe we weren't going to find common ground.

I think we were both pleasantly surprised to find that neither of us hated it. In fact, parts of what we experienced that morning seemed to speak to both of us. Was it a one-off fluke, or had the Card of Destiny truly delivered us to our future church home?

What it Takes, and Gives

I can skip to the end of the story and spoil the cliffhanger for you. As of this writing in 2020, our family has called His Hands our church home for more than a decade. But the full Appreciation here is a much larger revelation.

One interesting thing about the Appreciation process is that it doesn't exist on a set timeline. Honestly, there are only so many things in your life that are going to take you through all four stages of Seeing, Getting, Giving Thanks, and Growing What You Got. Whether or not you get all the way there and how long it takes to arrive depends on the situation itself, the decisions you make, the actions you take, and the perspective you apply along the way.

In His Hands, I could see the beginning of the value almost immediately. But I had no way of knowing how that value would grow and appreciate over time. In the very first conversation we had about our experience I could tell there was a fire of hope in Carie that we might have found an answer to a challenge that was critically important to her.

Let's stop there for a minute. This isn't a book at all about how to foster a happy, lasting marriage – but let me give you one tip. When you see that something is truly important to someone you love, please understand; there is enormous value in figuring out how you can help be part of making it happen for them. Those are the things in life that are actually *worth* Appreciating.

So, I knew church was important to Carie. Finding one that served both our needs would absolutely strengthen our marriage. But that value extended well beyond just the two of us, eventually paying dividends in our children and the relationships we'd continue to build with our family and friends.

Understanding that something is worth pursuing is relatively easy and doesn't require that much of us. Often, we get as far as understanding something and decide we're not willing or interested in pursuing it. We do these cost-benefit analyses all the time in life, trying to determine if what something TAKES will be worth what it GIVES. Sometimes the answer is no, and that's fine. Honestly, not everything we see or think is worth pursuing. But when the answer is "yes," and when we decide consciously to accept a challenge or work toward that thing of value, that's when we gain the necessary context to Appreciate it fully from the other side.

In this instance, that process took YEARS. Of course, there were instant payoffs of finding a church we agreed on. We stopped having The Conversation (and its related arguments) around whether such a thing was possible or something we were willing to work together to solve. We started encountering new ideas we could discuss together. And we were meeting new people. That brings us to another crossroads and one more way in which Carie and I are very different.

Another Break in the Wall

In general, I am outgoing socially, but risk-averse. By contrast, Carie is less gregarious and more willing to take risks. I'm often satisfied with the status quo, accepting change more out of necessity than desire. Carie is wired to embrace opportunities – especially in the interest of personal or professional growth.

So, after just a few weeks of attending this new church, when there was a discussion of Small Groups as part of the service, Carie's response was, "We should find a group to join." But my internal cynic flew into panic mode. *'What? We're going to church. I said yes to that. Now, you want me to dive deeper, join a Bible study or prayer group, be vulnerable, and engage with strange people I don't even know about religion and God? I definitely DON'T APPRECIATE THAT!'*

Here, "I don't appreciate that" means "that makes me very uncomfortable. I don't want to do that." And I really didn't want to. But I did. In hindsight, I absolutely appreciate Carie nudging me in the right direction. As you're starting to see, it's a dynamic that plays itself out time and again.

We did, in fact, go to an information meeting that next week about Small Groups. That led to us realizing there were other families with young children in our church looking to find support, kinship, and fellowship. We took another leap of faith and decided to attend a gathering of one such group, which ultimately led to us meeting several couples we still count among some of our best friends today. Ten plus years later, we've vacationed together, seen a few new babies born, and watched as those children have grown up in a sort of a Small Group of their own. The oldest of that group of children was seven when we met him. He began college this past fall and is one of the kindest, most Godly young men we know and an excellent mentor for our kids.

Of course, we're all grateful for having friends, and I do feel this way about those people. But the level of thanksgiving I feel for that small group of families goes well beyond the basic joy of merely meeting some lovely new people. These folks have become confidants, accountability partners, teachers, and more in our lives. One of them even baptized both of our children. I could stop there, and I would be grateful enough for what The Card of Destiny had brought into my life. But there were plenty of other blessings to come.

Growing What I Got

Throughout the years, we've become increasingly involved in various initiatives through His Hands Church. Carie and I both started volunteering. We began helping with the children's check-in team, which helped introduce us to the people and programs the church wrapped around its sizable youth population. From there, we both started working with kids about the same ages as ours (at that time, about 3 and 1).

We also became aware of other opportunities to help on a broader, community-based level. We got to participate in programs that bless underserved youth and families in our local area. We got plugged into a statewide resource network that provides ongoing assistance to families with emergent needs. We joined a team sponsoring children's and community programs in Guatemala. And we became involved with the ministry that helps serve the hundreds of foster children in our state. In these ways and more, we've also gotten a chance to understand, practice, and see the fruits of tithing (not just money, but time and talents) and to be blessed in return for being generous and faithful.

In truth, these are all just opportunities – crossroads that come with a choice. Choosing to engage and putting ourselves in a place of uncertainty or even discomfort, is what in this case, made it possible for me to Appreciate those opportunities fully. Only after I had SEEN, GOT, and become GRATEFUL for all those things, was I able to purposefully DO something with the knowledge and experiences I had gained. Now, I was empowered to GROW what I had gotten.

Here, it's helpful to remember that the first three stages of the Appreciation process are gifts TO you, whether you recognize them as such or not. Remember the example of the Empty Cup I described in the story of my friend Kevin's battle with cancer? Here it is again, with some added context.

It's true that you can't pour anything from that empty cup. But the process of *seeing* and *getting* starts to fill us. Being *grateful* for something takes us to the point of our cup almost overflowing. It's here that you have to share what you got or risk it being wasted.

And so, we dug in a little deeper. Instead of just tithing out of habit and being disconnected to any specific outcome those contributions might have, we created what we call a "God Fund." We still tithe, but in addition, we set aside a sum each month that goes into a separate fund. These funds don't belong to us. They belong to God and are available to serve His needs, on His time, when and where His Spirit leads us. Sometimes there is a little in that cup, and sometimes it's overflowing, but there's always something in it for us to pour out when God shows us a need to address. God has shown us time and again that the real value of money is the good that one can do with it to help others. That's a lesson we're able to live out consistently by faithfully listening for His voice to direct us. It's also one we're able to share with our kids about the value and power of being faithfully generous with our blessings.

We found other opportunities to serve and even lead – a prospect I would never have imagined before the Card of Destiny arrived. Would you believe that within a couple of short years, the guy who wanted nothing to do with going to church would be helping lead a team that shared the Word and love of God by providing Christmas presents for hundreds of local children? It's true.

Our involvement with the children's programs continued to grow as well. Carie dug in deeper there too, using her natural love for children and her talents in curriculum development to pursue the creation of a Vacation Bible School program. My volunteer path followed our kids. As they progressed from pre-school and elementary through to junior- and senior high school programs, I stayed with them. Along that path, I've gotten to see and actively participate in the spiritual development of our own children, and hundreds of others in their same age groups, throughout basically their entire childhoods. To those kids, who, as of this writing are 11-17 years old, I'm probably "that old, grey dude," but I've actually developed genuine relationships with a lot of them. I try hard to appreciate those.

Most Sundays come and go without a lot of earth-shattering revelations. But on several occasions, I've been blessed to connect with, relate to, or share (a non-parent, adult) perspective with a young person in a way that might even have a lasting impact. Knowing a kid got the advice, encouragement, or even just the safe, non-judgmental company they needed – things they might not have gotten if you weren't there that day – is a gift beyond measure. Those are gifts that keep filling the cup. I know for sure that working with those kids and hearing their stories (some of which are identical to our kids', and some of which are entirely, heartbreakingly different) equips me to be a better parent. There's no better application of me literally *growing what I've got*.

Knowing that your own kids are getting the same from other people you trust (who aren't THEIR parents) is an incredible gift too. Almost the entire leadership of our church consists of people younger than me. In fact, many of the junior high and high school leaders are half my age, but most of them have twice my spiritual knowledge and surety. Watching those young people teach other young people and be utterly relatable in a way I never could is amazing. I try to remember every Sunday to thank my fellow volunteers. In general, I'm thanking them for the opportunity to work with them, which I truly enjoy. But more often than not, I find myself thanking them for teaching ME too. I've stopped being surprised by how often and how much I can learn from people much younger than me. They are constantly filling my cup to ensure I have something of value to give to someone else and helping me GROW and truly Appreciate the many gifts the Card of Destiny has given to me.

Maybe this is the natural postscript to this particular chapter, or perhaps I'm just saving the best part for last here. A few years after we started attending His Hands regularly, and long after we became invested in staying, we talked with a staff member. He told me everything I needed to know about how Carie and I actually got there. This person asked us how long we had been coming to the church, and how we first discovered it. Basic questions, right? We told him that a few years back, right as the church was launching in its new building, we received one of those postcards in our mailbox at random. His next question was logical enough too. "Where do you guys live?" His reaction to our response was pure amazement. Remember that 25-minute drive I told you about, the one that seemed not much of a big deal to us? He thought for a second and then said something I'll never forget. "I was part of that project. I know how many postcards we sent and exactly where we sent them. I can tell you with 100% certainty; we didn't send *any* postcards as far away as your house – like literally ZERO to your ZIP Code." Now it was our turn to be amazed. *Somebody* sent the Card of Destiny to our house that day. I can totally Appreciate that He did.

Questions to Consider:

• When in your life have you known for sure you were led to the right place, at exactly the right time, possibly even beyond (or even despite) your own efforts?

• What blessing came from that serendipity?

• Have you ever thanked God and the people involved for putting you there?

• How have you Appreciated the blessings you received?

Wisdom to Appreciate:

Jeremiah 29:11 - "For I know the plans I have for you, declares the Lord, plans for welfare and not for evil, to give you a future and a hope."

1 Chronicles 16:11 - "Seek the Lord and his strength; seek his presence continually!"

1 John 4:1 - "Beloved, do not believe every spirit, but test the spirits to see whether they are from God, for many false prophets have gone out into the world."

Chapter 6:
Building a Foundation

In 2010, our oldest son was five years old and beginning kindergarten. Like all parents taking their first child to school, the whole experience was new for us. We had neighbors whose older children were already at the school. But aside from getting a few insights into who they thought were the "nice" or "good" teachers, we were pretty much going in cold.

Orientation

To get the lay of the land and see what life might be like for our new student, we attended orientation. A standard feature of those meetings is exposing families to the many ways they can help support their school. There are spirit items to purchase, committees to join, and volunteer opportunities a-plenty.

At orientation, many people join the PTA, paying a small membership sum in the process. For most, that brief interaction is one of the few times they think about the PTA or those various other groups. Especially as a first-time parent, you might be grateful that *someone* is doing those crucial jobs. But at the same time, you're kind of glad it's not YOU who's doing it. On this level, you can see such groups exist, but you haven't recognized their value enough to appreciate it just yet.

I lived in that reality for a year or so. I was perfectly happy to let those other smart, motivated people make plans affecting my child, without any real need to be part of it.

By Matt's second year of elementary school (our youngest, Liam, was two years behind, still in pre-K), we had figured out enough to relax and process things differently. We started to see what it looked like to get involved and saw several opportunities to do so.

Around this time, we became aware of another organization that had just started at our school – an educational Foundation. Like the PTA, and intended to work in partnership with it, the Foundation was a group of parents and faculty shareholders united in improving the students' educational experience. Unlike the PTA, though, the Foundation focused on raising funds to address the school's capital improvement needs. Such an organization had been proposed in the past. Still, it wasn't actually born until a particular group of motivated parents decided to do the hard work of establishing it from the ground up.

I hadn't really seen the PTA as a place to get involved. But there was something different and more appealing about the Foundation. That is not to say I immediately jumped in and started serving. Some of our friends had, though. Taking cues from other schools, they researched how to build a Foundation from scratch and then basically cobbled together a fledgling organization out of whole cloth.

When we talked with these friends socially, the conversation inevitably turned to our kids and their school. In that casual way, we came to learn about the Foundation and its goals. We discovered it was a place where people we already knew and liked worked together to do something useful and valuable for our kids and the community. That fledgling nature of the organization - established but still in its infancy - was a bit of a draw, too. Plus, most of the members were already our friends, so it seemed like an "easy" fit. In full disclosure, I do mean that in both senses of the word "easy." It was both comfortable and not a ton of responsibility. At that point, it was "easy" to show up to a meeting with your friends once or twice a month and say, "that sounds good, how can I help?" about plans I didn't have much of a stake or responsibility in having made. I was very much just dipping my toes in the shallow end of volunteering at my kids' school – which was at least a start, I guess.

Carie and I both got involved with the Foundation that year, and only then did I even begin to see what might lie ahead. There were plenty of opportunities, but as many or more obstacles too.

Here, I should mention that our school was designated a Title 1 School, which means that a significant portion of the student population was economically challenged. While the neighborhood our family lived in was solidly middle class, our school zone included several low-income communities as well. There are both challenges and blessings in that reality. One natural by-product of our school's zoning was a high degree of racial and cultural diversity. Carie and I were always grateful for this, as integration with people from diverse backgrounds is something we see as wholly positive for our kids. From a logistical standpoint, though, there were barriers, not the least of which was language. The school and its organizations had to be able to communicate in several languages or risk having no dialog with significant portions of the population. The other reality of a Title 1 School is that, to some degree, it sets the tone for what is meant by "capital improvements." For some schools, those with more affluent populations and better connections, capital improvements might be a shiny, new athletic complex, performing arts theater, or a state-of-the-art computer lab. As we became more familiar with our Foundation, I learned that our goals were considerably more modest.

Now, recall, this is a nearly-new organization, starting with literally zero funding and next to no awareness in the school or community. In the beginning, people didn't know we even existed, let alone what we were working to accomplish. That we were able to buy new blinds for the cafeteria and get a working refrigerator and microwave donated for the teachers' lounge were big successes. We worked diligently, chipping away at the awareness issue. We made ourselves seen and heard as we crossed off small, short-term needs while trying to sock away funds for more formidable long-range goals.

The first of those long-term goals was to replace the worn and frankly, gross carpeted flooring our students had in their gymnasium. In our first year of involvement with the Foundation, I remember being sure that this need would be taken care of as part of the series of SPLOST initiatives funded by taxes on the community. And, I remember being incredulous at seeing our little needy school passed over in favor of a much larger and more well-funded school's "need" for a new multi-million dollar facility on its campus.

And so it went for two years. The Foundation's leadership was solid, dedicated, and smart. We forged partnerships with the school's administration and PTA, and the organization grew by logical baby steps, gaining new members and growing in terms of awareness and knowledge. Finally, at the end of that second year, with the help of more SPLOST dollars, we were able to replace that nasty gym carpeting with a new alternative that improved our students' recreational experience and health.

Having checked off our big long-term goal, we started looking at new major capital improvement opportunities. It was around this time that one of our members suggested that the next big need was obvious. The school had two playgrounds, one appropriate for kids in kindergarten through 2nd grade, and one better suited for 3rd through 5th grades. Both were already aged, and neither had any ADA-compliant options for special needs students, another population our school served. Since the playground for the older kids was much worse for wear, replacing it became our next major goal.

Remember that gym flooring? The one it took two years to replace? That cost was somewhere around $20,000. The first estimate we got for a new playground? $85,000! By now, our kids were about to finish 2nd grade and kindergarten, and I recall thinking – *"Great. We can work on that, but my kids are NEVER gonna touch or even see this new playground."* That thought was honest, but very cynical.

At this point, Carie and I had worked with the Foundation for two years. We attended meetings, gave input, took jobs with various committees, helped out with numerous fundraisers, and did our best to spread the word about the organization. I had now been there long enough to *see* the Foundation for what it was and involved from the inside long enough to *get* it. I knew how the Foundation worked, and in a general sense, I DID appreciate the good things it achieved. And I had some sense of accomplishment from being "involved." But I was still pretty firmly planted on the sidelines – perfectly willing to help when asked, but not really in charge of anything. Then, as it does, everything changed.

Thrown Under the School Bus

As that school year ended, we learned that the Foundation's first President intended to step down. He'd done a remarkable job leading the organization's creation, establishing connections with administration, and recruiting a small group of focused and passionate people to join. In his time there, the Foundation took root and showed it could set and achieve short and long-term goals. He had also weathered the transition between one Principal (a twenty-plus year veteran moving into retirement) and her replacement (a younger, highly motivated professional with a vision and style all her own). The outgoing President had done the Foundation proud and set it up for even greater success. The question now was – who was going to lead moving forward?

I didn't have to wait long to find out. A few weeks later, Carie and I were at a friend's house – coincidentally gathered with several of our neighbors who served with us on the Foundation. Predictably, the conversation turned to talk of kids and school. We were making small talk when one of the ladies came right out and said to me – "We think YOU should be the next President of the Foundation." I don't think I even had time to consider whether it was a joke or not. Nor did it occur to me to ask exactly who this "we" was that had decided this. To my continuing horror, Carie pretty quickly endorsed the idea, too.

To say I DIDN'T APPRECIATE THAT would be an understatement. In the moment, it felt more like equal parts being drafted and nominated. Here, "I don't appreciate that" translates roughly into "well, that's not at all what I want." What I'm sure I wanted at that moment was for things to go on just as they had. I wanted to be involved but not in charge.

The prospect of being responsible for something much larger than just me and which potentially impacted hundreds of people – most of whom were elementary-aged children – was kind of terrifying. I don't like letting people down. The prospect of failing in an endeavor like that was most definitely "not what I wanted."

I made some meek objections about not being qualified for such a task, but the group wasn't having it. Several of them were already officers in the Foundation and assured me I would be a good fit. And so, reluctantly – or more accurately, with great hesitation and trepidation – I accepted the challenge.

At that time, had I been looking for it, I would have found solace in the wisdom and security we get from Isaiah 42:16 – *"And I will lead the blind in a way they do not know, in paths that they have not known I will guide them. I will turn the darkness before them into light, the rough places into level ground."*

I was definitely headed blindly down an unknown path. A wiser, more secure person might have embraced the comfort of being led by Providence in such a situation. I wasn't there yet, but thankfully, He still leads those who follow reluctantly.

One thing I did know about leadership though is that a leader's success often depends on the quality of people supporting them. I also knew that in situations where I personally felt supported (i.e., had a safety net against failure), I felt much better about myself and typically gained better results.

So, I did have some confidence here, knowing that if I were going to take on this role and serve as a leader, I would be well supported. The other Foundation officers had been there since its inception, and I had seen firsthand how well they kept things organized and moving forward. They knew far more than I did and would be a wealth of knowledge and good advice.

All of this was good because there were plenty of decisions to make. I have always considered myself a person who "enjoys" politics – or at least the idea of trying to bring people together who have different ideas about how to do things. But I'd never had any real practice at it. I'm not suggesting the Foundation was political, in function, or even nature. But I was about to get a crash course in figuring out how to build coalitions among groups with very different agendas.

That course began even before my "administration." In the first meeting of the new school year, with most of the regular Foundation group in attendance, we explained that the former President had stepped down over the summer and that I had accepted the post. What didn't occur to me until right then was that my "nomination" and my subsequent "inauguration" had taken place in our friend's kitchen and were anything but formal. The decision to install me as President had included the Foundation's remaining officers, but not all of its stakeholders. A few people found out for the first time at that meeting that leadership had changed without their knowledge. Not surprisingly, they didn't *appreciate* that. It wasn't that they had any specific animosity towards me, lacked confidence in the Board's decision, or even disagreed with it. They just really would have liked to have been consulted beforehand. Their feelings were something I hadn't considered, but which I totally understood in hindsight. I don't think anyone caught off guard was actually angling to do the job themselves, so those issues were easy enough to smooth over. But it was a powerful lesson for me about needing to do things "the right way," communicating openly, and always trying to build consensus.

From there, other new bridges needed building, too. Our Principal was already supportive of the organization, so that one was easy enough. Others were more challenging. The Foundation still struggled to communicate effectively and to gain traction, even within the school itself. Some of the teachers still didn't even know who we were or what we were trying to do (for them and the students). More than anything, this was an awareness challenge. In general, teachers want what is best for their school and their students. Simply introducing ourselves and helping them understand our goals and how those plans would benefit the work they did every day, that went a long way.

The PTA was another bridge that needed building and improving. They were already well-entrenched and very visible, whereas the Foundation had only existed for two years at this point. I had never really considered the school calendar from a "political" perspective. The more familiar I became with how events were planned, the more I saw how complex it could be. The PTA had a very well-organized schedule of events, spread strategically throughout the year. And, until the creation of the Foundation, they were the only organization working on behalf of the school. As we began to plan ways to achieve our goals (which required significant fundraising), I began to learn that at least in some ways, the Foundation might be viewed as "the competition."

It mattered that our mission was different from theirs. Ours was to raise funds for things the PTA wasn't even legally allowed to do. But from a different perspective, we were still a new kid on the block, now "competing" for the finite (and very limited) resources of the school population's time, interest, and money. We were all working for the same thing – making the school a better place for our teachers and kids. But it made sense on some level that even our sister organization might not *appreciate* having to make room at a table they'd previously had all to themselves.

And then there was the community at large. That bridge didn't even fully exist yet. We knew there were opportunities for partnerships, sponsorships, and grants. And we knew these resources were critical if we were to succeed in our ambitious plans for the school. But this was a bridge for another day. Getting our internal house in order was more pressing and plenty enough of a challenge at the outset.

Getting familiar with the lay of the land, the various relationships at play, and how all of those pieces would fit together helped me appreciate the situation on a whole new level. This is where gratitude starts to become a factor. To fully embrace a leadership role in the Foundation, I would have to put myself out there. I would have to be vulnerable. And I would have to admit that I was going to need a LOT of help. Some of it would come naturally from people I knew, trusted, and who already shared my goals. Some of it would have to come from people I didn't know yet – people I had to convince that our plans were worthy of their support. And some of it would have to come from people who might even be predisposed to think we were an obstacle to their own separate goals.

That process of figuring out how to partner with other people, on a scale that size, was very much an exercise in gratitude and empathy. In each of those relationships, I had to understand what the other people wanted or needed before proposing a way for the Foundation to help create a mutual benefit.

The more conversations I had, the more I started to see the impact of effectively communicating our goals and mission. The Principal offered blanket support for our goals and was willing to lend an open ear and her valuable time to advise us. Teachers became supporters, ready to distribute information about our initiative and to volunteer at our events. The PTA became a real partner, opening their monthly meetings to us for continued visibility and a platform for communication. They were even willing to make space in the calendar to empower our fundraising efforts.

In each scenario, we had to approach these various audiences and ask for more than we could give in return on the promise that, with their help, eventually, the long-term result would be a great win-win for everyone. A proposition like that is always a leap of faith. But remarkably, in every instance, the people we approached said YES. And with every yes came another infusion of gratitude – true gratefulness that people believed in what we were trying to do and were willing to help. Along with gratitude, this support brought confidence and a belief that maybe some of those ambitious things we had planned might just be possible.

Getting Invested

As all the pieces began to fall into place, and the bridges got built, we dug in and started doing the actual work. As with any organization experiencing a leadership transition, we knew some things were already working and effective. At the same time, we were definitely looking for new ways to grow, communicate, and raise money. We talked at length about various fundraisers and had many brainstorming sessions about how to chip away at the mountainous goal ahead of us.

Remember, as a Title 1 school, our population wasn't flush with wealthy benefactors just waiting to stroke big checks. We had a few "partners in education" in the corporate community, but usually, these were sort of symbiotic relationships. Partners like local restaurant franchises would happily host Spirit Nights, donating 10% of sales to our organization. Those did genuinely help our bottom line, for which we were grateful. But it was probably a better deal in total for them than it was for us. Events like these, and standards like bake sales and seasonal item sales, were mainstays of our fundraising efforts. But we'd been doing things like that long enough to see about how much money they generated. We were essentially trying to nickel-and-dime our way to an $80,000 playground – a somewhat demoralizing prospect.

Our current efforts were making small gains. But if we were going to meet our very ambitious goal, our ideas and actions would need to be equally ambitious and creative.

Up to that point, we had been working hard, but probably in only one direction relative to fundraising. What truly made a difference was when collectively, we started looking at some completely new ideas – and listening to a lot of different voices with open ears and minds. Tons of creative ideas, ranging wildly in scope and seriousness, got tossed around in our meetings. Without the ability and willingness of those people to explore and try new things, we'd have been stuck going nowhere fast.

One of these ideas was to embrace the concept of nickel-and-diming literally. We installed a 100-gallon glass aquarium in the school's lobby, inviting anyone who entered to donate their spare change (or dollars) to our cause. We divided it into six sections (one for each grade) and created a friendly competition to see which grade could raise the most money, with a party to reward the winners. Over two years, we probably pulled close to $3,000 out of that tank, just by putting an opportunity in peoples' paths and offering a fun way for the kids to get involved. This initiative also gave me one of the strongest illustrations of "investment" I've ever seen.

When a 7-year-old child tells you they are donating their allowance to their school's Foundation because "other people need this more than I do," you're doing more than just raising money. You're literally planting seeds of appreciation. Giving the students the opportunity to participate in their success was a huge revelation. And getting to see those kids practice concepts like charity and empathy might have been a win that equaled getting the playground itself.

Another path we explored was hosting fundraising events of our own. We had friends from another school who told us about the annual Bingo Night their school hosted. They canvased the community soliciting prize donations and raised money via admission to the event, bingo cards, and concessions. We'd never tried anything like it, but our friends had a really solid plan we were able to follow as a template, so we dove in and went for it.

Carie jumped in to chair this new committee, working with our friends to adapt their template to our needs, and everyone else manned the numerous tasks required to pull off such an event. We pounded the pavement for months in search of donations, and though we didn't have a 100% success rate, it was incredibly gratifying to see how often people were willing to help. This process was a giant reminder for me of the truth that "you never know unless you ask." The worst thing that could happen when you asked for help was that someone would say "no," in which case, you were no worse off than when you started. Conversely, with every "yes" came a new rush of gratitude, excitement, and confidence. It probably took us six months of planning to pull off that event, but at the end of the day, our inaugural Bingo Night raised around $5,000 – a quantum leap in not only our funds but also in our thinking about how we raised them.

By my second year, we'd gained some serious traction. People (certainly inside the school, but also increasingly in the community) knew that we existed. They knew who we were and what we were trying to do. And in many instances, they knew how to help us. Starting from next to nothing, we'd amassed a five-figure balance that allowed us to keep funding small, short-term improvements while continuing to chip away at the mountain of our big goal. It was cool to think we'd figured out how to grow from nickels-and-dimes to $20,000+, but also daunting to remember our goal of $80,000+ was still really nowhere in sight.

Success on a Whole New Level

Our exploration of alternate fundraising ideas also took us down another exciting, new path. One of our members, a wonderful lady named Kate, worked with a local charity. Out of pure necessity in her job there, she became aware of writing grant proposals. This process gave her a whole new understanding of and appreciation for the impact of private charitable contributions. This possibility wasn't even on my radar.

As President, I suppose I should have been tirelessly searching for every way possible to achieve our goals. And in some ways, I was. But one of the things I love about my experience with the Foundation is how much it helped me recognize and appreciate the power of teamwork. Nobody is good at everything. Usually, when people try to be, or worse, think they already are, the results are predictably awful. Conversely, when you assemble a team of smart, hard-working people who have complementary skills, the ceiling is nearly limitless.

I know for sure that without Kate, the idea – and definitely the practice – of soliciting charitable grants is something I would never have pursued on behalf of the Foundation. It made absolute sense, and from what we could see, there was a long list of benefactors both nationally and locally offering money every year to organizations just like ours. But the process of filling out those (often massive) applications only for the chance to be considered among the countless other folks vying for the same help? Again, paralyzingly daunting.

So, when Kate suggested we start applying for grants, I was enthusiastic, but guardedly so. I was ecstatic to have someone who knew about that stuff, who could lead us toward potentially colossal success in a way I knew I never could. In several ways, I was the person out front for the Foundation, speaking publicly to teachers and parents, soliciting business owners for donations, etc. But on this front, I was right back to being a cheerleader on the sidelines. And honestly, I was just fine with that. I knew

NOTHING about writing grants, let alone doing it well enough to succeed at it. Kate enthusiastically and confidently took that ball and ran with it, knowing I'd do whatever I could to help her.

For months, we'd have regular Board meetings. At each, we'd get updates on fundraising in general, various initiatives we were working on, and the status of our grant applications. We had a few irons in the fire there, but most of those applications suggested lengthy timetables for consideration. So, we went about our business of mining nickels and dimes, staying hopeful we'd hear something encouraging about a larger windfall.

A few weeks later, I went to the local Post Office, where the Foundation maintained a P.O. Box. We'd done a letter-writing campaign, which was still getting some replies, so I checked the box regularly. On that day, I opened it and found a letter from one of the several charitable organizations I knew that we'd solicited for a grant. It was a simple, thin envelope. My cynical nature told me that, like most of the job applications or publishing queries I'd submitted, this envelope would contain a short, sweet rejection letter. They would thank us for our time and interest but ultimately wish us better luck in someone else's pasture. I was profoundly wrong.

I had waited until I got home from the Post Office to open the mail, and I'm glad I did. That letter informed me our recent grant application was *accepted* and that the organization was pledging $38,900 toward our goal. At first, I was in shock. Then, I started crying, literally overcome with emotion at the prospect of delivering on our vision to bring a new playground to the hundreds of students at our little Title 1 school. Within minutes, I called both Carie and Kate. Still choking back tears, I shared the fantastic news I still couldn't quite believe was true.

At this point, on the grand spectrum of appreciation, I had already traveled most of the way. Long ago, I had SEEN it, and I definitely GOT what the organization could potentially do. The process of working with new people to figure out new ways to accomplish those goals gave me gratitude. I was extremely thankful for the support and cooperation of so many people who brought skills to the table I simply didn't have. All that was left, for me to fully Appreciate this opportunity was to figure out how to GROW what I was given.

Getting All the Way There

In this situation, what I had been "given" was an organization with a solid foundation and established goals, a group of people willing and more than capable of accomplishing those goals, and the mutual trust among people with diverse talents to do what needed to be done. You can't ask for much more, and in hindsight, it's easy to see why we succeeded.

The joy of getting that letter lasted a while, but it wouldn't take me long to realize that even with that nearly $40K infusion, we were still roughly $15,000 short of the playground. Now, with half our need pledged from an outside donor, and about a quarter of it sitting in our account – a sum it had taken us two-plus years to raise – we faced the prospect of trying to raise the remaining quarter in just a few months before the current school year ended.

So, we did one more thing we'd never done before. We went to the Principal with a proposal. We desperately wanted this playground for these kids, and now, we were so close (but still far enough away) that it hurt. It was time to go back to the lesson of that fish tank in the lobby. On a small scale, that tank had shown both adults and kids how they could personally contribute to making a huge impact. We asked the Principal for permission to launch a capital campaign that would push us over the finish line. We did some basic math and figured out that our total need equaled about $35 per family at the school. Surely, on the heels of learning we'd been granted $40K, our families would rally and push us over the line, right? Maybe.

We had plenty of discussions, most in the context of our population's limited resources. Many were already receiving free or reduced lunches, and for most of them, $35 in expendable income probably wasn't a reality. We had to try, though.

We held a pep rally for the students, announcing to a full cafeteria of children that we had received a gift of nearly $40,000 and that a new playground was closer than ever. Predictably, they cheered with great excitement. When we told them we still needed a little bit of help to get all the way there, they were still enthusiastic. But how would their parents react?

They did exactly as we hoped. Remember the 2nd-grade student who once told me, "other people need this more than I do?" Similarly, the parents, students, teachers, and faculty all dug deep. And with just a few weeks of school left, we officially raised the rest of what we needed to buy a brand new, ADA-compliant playground for those kids.

In the end, over that two-year journey, the Foundation went from being a stable yet fledgling organization on a shoe-string budget, to raising over $80,000. More importantly, we also managed to empower even the youngest members of that community to see our goal as something in which they could and should want to share ownership.

Over that summer, we broke ground and installed a brand-new playground for hundreds of kids at one little school in Marietta, GA. When they returned for the new school year, we had a ribbon-cutting ceremony celebrating our success. I was there, and proudly so, but no longer front or center. Just as securing that playground was a mile marker in our journey with the Foundation, Carie and I had determined our road was taking us elsewhere in other ways. We had decided that after 13 years, the time had come to sell our home. That move would mean a change of schools for our boys and another leadership change for the Foundation. With our largest goal, and several other small ones, accomplished, I was ready to pass the baton.

At that ceremony, Kate, our illustrious grant writer, and the single biggest reason those kids got that new playground, rightfully presided as the new President of Foundation. She was the perfect person to begin a new era of growth for both the group and the school.

Here's the irony, though. Remember how my "administration" began – with an impromptu inauguration in our friend's kitchen? I was a volunteer who was "volun-told" they were about to become a leader. Two years later, even knowing exactly how little I appreciated that tactic, I basically passed the torch to Kate in the same way. She did get much more advanced warning of the bus she was being thrown under, though. She became Vice President after our first year working together. Quickly after that, I started telling her regularly what a great President she was going to make when I stepped down. She saw the bus coming from a long way off and probably had plenty of time to get out of the way if she had wanted to. Instead, she hopped right on and grabbed the wheel with both hands. What did she do with her "volun-told" opportunity? Kate would steer the Foundation for several more years, achieving great success and earning much-deserved recognition as the County's Volunteer of the Year following the playground installation.

As I think back on that journey, I realize that what I was truly given in that situation was an opportunity. I got the chance to work hard for something bigger than myself, for the benefit of my own children and hundreds of others. I got to meet and work alongside some of the nicest, smartest, and hardest-working people I've ever known. I got to learn a little bit about leadership. And, I got to grow as a person.

But most importantly, I got to grow what others had given me. Like all material things, that playground will become old and run down one day and need replacing. For me, though, it will always stand as a symbol of something I had no idea just how much I could Appreciate.

I'm sure it's possible for one person to singularly plow their way to achieving a goal with only their own vision and efforts. But it seems far more likely that teams of people with different abilities and knowledge, united in a common mission, will ultimately create far greater success. This was certainly the case with our Foundation.

I haven't been in many leadership positions, but I probably UNDER-appreciate how easy I had it as President of that group. Because we were a volunteer organization, I assume everyone was there out of desire and not some other sense of obligation. We may have had some disagreements along the way, but mostly we were aligned, and trust was never an issue. I'm sure a lot of what we did in those few years was sort of commonplace, but the outcome was exceptional because so were the people and their passion.

In the same way, I clearly underappreciated the truth in the words of Isaiah. In real time, I wasn't even noticing where God had placed me – blindly starting down a path, without clarity, toward rough places that would need to be leveled. Now, through experiences like the ones I've had with the Foundation, I'm thankfully a little less blind and lot more willing to follow His lead.

It wouldn't be until our family moved to that different school district – one with a completely different economic reality – that I would be able to fully appreciate the challenges our Foundation faced and the successes we were able to achieve. At the orientation for our youngest child's new elementary school – one with a gymnasium sponsored by the local NBA team – we got a pledge form. It suggested quite succinctly that if each family just wrote a check for $1,000 right then, there would be no need for additional solicitations throughout the year. I'm not exactly sure I appreciated that invitation. And when the time came to write a check, I didn't.

- In your associations and relationships, are you merely "involved" or truly INVESTED?

- When have you been asked to do something beyond your level of preparation, comfort, or desire?

- In the transition from seeing challenge to recognizing opportunity, what was the breakthrough?

- In what challenges have you been given the opportunity to recognize and appreciate skills other people have that you might lack?

- Think about your successes. Compare how much there is to appreciate in individual triumphs vs. team efforts.

Wisdom to Appreciate:

Proverbs 3:5-6 - Trust in the Lord with all your heart, and do not lean on your own understanding. In all your ways acknowledge him, and he will make straight your paths.

Isaiah 42:16 - And I will lead the blind in a way that they do not know, in paths that they have not known I will guide them. I will turn the darkness before them into light, the rough places into level ground.

Chapter 7:
Fostering Appreciation

By this point, you've already heard me express gratitude several times for my lovely wife, Carie. I'm about to go there again, but that's okay. Gratitude and appreciation are limitless resources, which in my experience are akin to love; they only grow within you the more you give them away.

As I've said before, I firmly believe that almost all of the good things currently in my life are gifts that have come, directly or indirectly, from my relationship with Carie. This particular chapter of my life is undoubtedly one of those.

Carie has a remarkably huge heart for children. She shows it every day as an amazing mother to our own two boys. She also shares her gifts of love regularly as a volunteer in our church's pre-school classes. In fact, Carie often says that if she were to make a career change, she would trade her role as a successful executive in a heartbeat to start a daycare or school and work with kids full time. I don't doubt that for a second.

The other thing I have learned never to doubt, and have also previously mentioned, is that when Carie hears something from God, she listens – and I should, too. Like many of our other blessings, following her lead in faithfully heeding such a call is precisely how we got involved serving children in our state's foster system.

Answering a Call

Just as with our search for a church, Carie had a yearning to serve children in foster care, which she nurtured through patience and prayer until it became a clear calling. And once again, I was a few steps behind. In this instance, we both shared the same big heart for working with kids – although the applications were a little different. She volunteered in the church nursery, on committees at our kids' schools, and bravely dove in when our oldest son's Cub Scout troop needed leadership. I worked with slightly older kids at our church, headed our kids' school Foundation, and coached their baseball teams. We should have been in lockstep with each other around this opportunity to serve kids in an even more meaningful way. But the truth is, I was scared. I don't even know specifically what I feared. Maybe it was my (correct) assumption of the magnitude of need in the foster system. Perhaps it was my ignorance of how any of it worked. Between those and my own insecurities about serving in this space, fear had me stalled.

Carie and I occasionally had conversations about becoming foster parents, but honestly, it was a path I struggled to see. In her exploration of the foster landscape, she discovered the previously unknown opportunity to become respite foster parents – those who take children into their homes for short periods of time to give primary foster parents a much-needed break. This idea seemed more realistic, and was interesting, but still, I wasn't quite ready to jump in yet.

Less than a week after Carie first shared the idea of respite foster care, we received a call from our pastor. Again, God was making it clear it was time to get involved. Our pastor told us there was an urgent need to support a family inside our own church. After praying about who to contact, he was reaching out to see if we would consider joining in to serve and support a family whose children may soon enter foster care. He mentioned that another family had already stepped in to serve as primary foster parents if needed, but they would need more help, including respite foster families to come alongside them and provide support. The timing of the conversation, only days after Carie and I first discussed the possibility of providing respite foster care, seemed more than a coincidence.

A few days later, we attended a meeting at our church to learn more about Faithbridge, a foster care organization that was helping to organize our church's response. I recall being relieved upon walking into the room and discovering that we weren't alone in our interest. A decent number of people had assembled to learn more about the situation and possible solutions. That meeting only lasted about an hour, but it fundamentally changed my perception of the foster care system and our potential role in it. We listened as the founder of Faithbridge gave us a little historical background on the organization and then explained how they operate. He gave us a lot of information. But two things were crystallized for me and really got my attention. The first was a statistic – one that would genuinely startle my brain and break my heart. Here's what he told us:

"If every church in America would commit to taking care of just one foster child, there would be no foster children left in America."

Sit with that for just a minute.

He wasn't saying that every FAMILY in every church needed to take a foster child into their home personally. Rather, any CHURCH FAMILY could come together and more than meet any child's total needs. I'll get to the specifics of that in a minute, but let's go back to the original statement first. Here it is again:

If every CHURCH in America committed to taking care of just ONE foster child, there would be NO foster children left in America.

At face value, that doesn't even seem possible, but the numbers check out. That meeting happened a couple of years ago. At that time, there were right around 400,000 of each – churches and children in foster care across the United States. The number of churches didn't necessarily surprise me – they're readily visible on the streets of America every day. The number of foster kids shocked me, mostly because I'd probably never even considered what that number might be.

That statistic helped reinforce the original fear I brought to that meeting and most of my prior conversations with Carie. That's one HUGE problem. TOO big for my comfort. How in the world does one person even begin to make any real difference?

Phillipians 2:5-7 suggests a solution – *"In your relationships with one another, have the same mindset as Christ Jesus: who, being in very nature God, did not consider equality with God something to be used to his own advantage. Rather, he made himself nothing by taking on the very nature of a servant."*

God's answer, in a nutshell? Serve. But what does that look like?

As our speaker continued, he answered that very question. He had already gotten my attention by defining the problem we had all expressed interest in helping solve – a staggering number of kids in need. In that way, he also allowed me to begin to appreciate something by helping me recognize that it even existed. But that was just the first step down a long, challenging road that lay ahead.

Next, he started to share HOW their organization helped flatten that curve. And to be honest, that curve is really like a wall – a literal barrier that keeps most people from diving in to help, mostly out of the same fear and ignorance I had. He began to describe what he called a "community of care." In this model, the entire focus is on surrounding one foster child/family with MANY supportive people, each with different roles, talents, and responsibilities. The truth is, foster kids need foster PARENTS, but that's not even close to ALL they need. People stepping up to become full-time foster parents is critical, but it's only part of the total need. If you're like me, you might have never even thought about that. When many people think about foster care, they imagine it as an all-in, singular, you vs. the world situation. I've talked to enough foster parents to know that even with a ton of support, it can often still feel that way, but having others around you to help carry the load makes an indescribable difference.

That's where the community of care comes in. Start with that original premise of you, alone, thrown into the challenging situation of trying to care for a child whose story, history, and traumas you don't know. Terrifying, right? Now, add another family who is ready, willing, and equipped to walk alongside you in a supportive role. That's a little better. Now add folks who can help with transportation to and from doctor's appointments, family visits, respite stays, and other activities. Now add tutors and other specialized professionals, each with their unique abilities. Suddenly, you have a literal "community of care" around a child, sharing their talents to support their total needs. The full-time parent is still the primary point and hub of care. But now, there are also several more spokes in the wheel. And suddenly, there's an epiphany: *"Wow. I'm not in this completely alone."* And then quickly, another one: *"Wow! I think I can actually do this."* And then you DO, and it's life-changing – for everyone involved, especially the children.

I'm not sure that Carie needed the extra reassurance; that is to say, I'm sure she would have dove in headfirst even without it. But for me, it was crucial. I do believe that among the biggest barriers to people stepping into foster care are that sense of overwhelming scope and a basic fear of the unknown. It's not as if being told that "you're not alone" solves all of your problems instantly, but it definitely changes your perspective and your prospects.

We left that meeting with a whole new appreciation for foster care, and I mean that in multiple senses. Before that day, neither of us had proper context for the scope of the need. And our previous understanding of the resources available, and the potential roles we could play as part of the solution, was incomplete at best. Several days later, we learned that the family in need was no longer in jeopardy of having children in foster care – a blessing in its own right – but the meeting at church that day had opened our eyes to a need in our community that we could no longer ignore.

Along with another family from our church, Carie and I decided our greatest opportunity to help was in the role of respite care. As a respite family, you are providing part-time care for foster children that allows full-time foster parents to manage appointments, keep commitments for work and their biological kids, or just get a much-needed break from the stresses of life. Respite families are not full-time foster parents. Unlike full-time fosters, respite families typically know how long the children they take into their care will be there. These stays can be anywhere from a few hours to a week or more, depending on specific needs. But, like full-time fosters, respite families become the primary caretakers of the foster kids under their watch. They are also required to undergo the same background checks and home studies as full-time foster parents. And they must complete the same kinds and quantities of training each year to maintain their active certification within their state. This training is another blessing for which I had no idea just how much appreciation I would eventually gain.

There Are Things You Must Know

Think about all the things you do in life which require at least some, if not significant, training. Driving a car; flying a plane; legal gun ownership; practicing law, medicine, and many other professions. The list goes on and on. Guess what does NOT legally require any prior training. Children! Sort of.

That's not to say there aren't parental training courses; there are plenty if you so desire. But no laws *require* you to have any training at all before bringing your own biological kids into this world. However, there are many specific and very stringent laws demanding such training for prospective foster parents. That contradiction is not ideal, and it likely contributes to some other, more extensive issues, but I digress.

Perhaps you've heard the phrase, "you don't know what you don't know." Nowhere is this more applicable than when it comes to parental training. Some parents read lots of books in those nine months, trying to flatten the curve on what to expect. Some follow the advice of family or friends. Some do the same as, or the complete opposite of, their own parents. Others just "wing it" and do the best they can. What's true in every case, though, is that you never quite know exactly how you will react to any one of the thousands of possible parenting scenarios until you're in the moment. That's where training can make a huge difference.

As we prepared for our own kids' arrivals, Carie was definitely a reader. I used a combination of all the strategies listed above. During this preparation, no one is telling you that you *must* learn certain things. You might not even have anyone telling you specifically what you *should* learn to be a good parent. It's totally up to you to decide what you don't know, what you could know better, and what you want to focus on in your own training – if anything at all.

As you enter the foster system, people will absolutely tell you that you MUST know several things (basic first aid, CPR for adults, children, and infants, water safety, etc.). There are also a wealth of in-person and online training courses covering a massive and diverse range of topics, including some you never imagined you might need. Depending on the children you encounter, there may be physical, mental, developmental, social, or cultural realities unlike any you've seen before. This training is critical in helping foster parents learn and gain confidence in managing children's behavior and well-being without the benefit of history or specific context.

Together, these resources offer a broad and deep knowledge base for prospective foster parents, a base which frankly would benefit ALL parents. So, I guess I shouldn't be surprised that one of the most appreciable results of getting involved in foster care is the certainty I have that it has made me a better parent overall.

Through a Child's Eyes

Foster children come from hard places. Often, their lives are full of unhealthy relationships, and many have encountered various forms of neglect or abuse. Whether intentional or not, these traumas form layers of emotional scar tissue, which ultimately color those children's views of relationships and the world around them. Under those layers, though, is still a human soul with the same basic needs and desires. In this way, children from hard places are just like kids from stable homes. And even though, thank God, my children have not experienced those same traumas, they too struggle with discipline and peer pressure and unhealthy choices and less-than-great-influences.

Training to better understand the experiences of kids from hard places, along with the defense mechanisms and coping strategies those kids employ to deal with such trauma, is fascinating and heartbreaking. Learning techniques to manage or even help overcome the behaviors and mindsets that those experiences create can be life-changing for everyone involved. When you have brilliant pediatric psychologists explain to you WHY a child behaves as they do, what the behavior means, AND how to meet it with a positive reaction; that's good, and maybe even better than you think. Here, you've done more than simply appreciate (recognize) the child's circumstance. You've actually Appreciated (grown) your own parenting skill set. The dividend? An ability to improve your interactions and relationship with *all* children.

As a parent, coach, and youth volunteer my world is wonderfully full of kids. I can't count the number of times I have been able to use a strategy learned in foster care training to create a better outcome with a child struggling to make good choices, interact appropriately with others, or even just recognize their own self-worth. I can't imagine that many people dive into the world of foster care with the specific intention of helping THEMSELVES. Still, I can tell you for sure that (once again) I am a better person for having followed Carie's lead toward this calling. I hope and believe our two sons probably feel the same, too.

They were a few years younger – early grade schoolers – when we embarked on this journey, and while we did talk with them about our intentions to get involved in this ministry, they probably didn't have veto power in the process. In that regard, they were more like passengers in a vehicle driven by Carie and me. But they were also old enough to make real decisions about whether they wanted to engage with the process or just be "along for the ride." Much to our pleasure, and each in their unique ways, both boys jumped in and bought into the plan.

It is difficult for a child to welcome other "strange" children into their homes; to share their space, toys, or food - and especially their parents' time and attention. It's not surprising that many birth children struggle with this process, at least in the beginning. But children are remarkably resilient. For our kids, seeing others come into their home came with a basic understanding. On some level, they are with *us* because it wasn't safe for them to be with their own families. Even at a young age, a realization like that creates context and empathy. In those interactions, they develop a better understanding of the world outside themselves and a sense of their own blessings. Now, add to that an opportunity for them to learn to share those blessings – especially with people they may not develop long-term relationships with and who are in no position to repay their kindness in any way. There's significant Appreciation happening there. For Carie and me, the recognition of those blessings was thoroughly conscious. For our boys, I suspect it was more like planting seeds; little kernels of context and empathy that hopefully sprout, grow, and blossom into tools that positively impact their own future relationships.

And so far, I feel like I've only scratched the "selfish" surface, describing the parts of foster care that have benefitted me and my own family. This doesn't even begin to cover the real point of the endeavor – making a positive impact on the children and families living in foster care.

The nature of foster care, particularly in a respite role, is that children often come into your home with very little notice. They stay for a few days and then move on, either back to their primary foster home or another temporary stop. In our three years in service, we've hosted many children, usually in sibling pairs, for stays as short as one night and as long as a week. What's amazing about these experiences is what they revealed to me about the nature of "relationship." We tend to think of relationships as things that develop slowly and which deepen in intensity over time. That idea is generally true. But foster care has shown me something else that is, too.

The Ways We're Connected

"Relationship" is defined as "the way in which two or more concepts, objects, or people are connected." Perfect. In this construct, there is no sense of time. The depth and nuances of your connection with someone will undoubtedly evolve the longer you know and interact with them. But there is no set amount of time you must spend with a person, place, idea, or even God, to be "in relationship." I love how this corresponds to the foster children who have graced our home. We only spent a single day or night with some of them. But I can guarantee you they got 100% of our time, energy, and attention. And I don't suggest that in the sense of just watching them to make sure they were physically safe. I mean doing our best to shut down other distractions and focus intently on what these new little people in our house are doing and saying. And perhaps most importantly, trying to tune acutely into their needs. Are they hungry or ambivalent? Do they want to play or be left alone? Are they scared or strangely at ease? Do they need to push boundaries, exercise control, or be led?

Think about it. With your own children, you develop a strong sense of these things over time. You have a lifetime together to "figure out" how each other act, react, think, and work. Same with the other adults you meet, except there, you're not responsible for them. With foster children, you enter immediately into a relationship with someone (who's only in your home because their other relationships are unstable, unreliable, or unsafe), and you have to figure it all out on the fly, in real time. Imagine a first date, a job interview, a babysitting gig, a counseling session, and a play date all rolled up into one experience happening at the same time – and the person, or people, on the other side of the equation are 2, or 5, or 10 years old.

Now you start to see where the heightened focus on attention comes into play. The training I spoke of earlier is critical, and it starts to kick in almost instinctively. You begin looking for cues in the behavior of a child who might be too young, or frankly too traumatized, to explain to you why they are acting as they are. Sometimes those cues are easier to spot than others, but at least now you're actively looking for them. And that's maybe the most critical part. Imagine treating ALL of your interactions with this sense of hyper-focus. How much richer, healthier, and more rewarding could all our relationships be if we gave them this level of attention?

I know this extra focus is a blessing to me and part of a larger sense of Appreciation I've gained through our experience with foster care. Essentially, I'm using strategies I didn't even know existed previously to understand all of my relationships better. These insights help me recognize the importance of things I'm seeing and hearing from other people. And that extra focus ultimately increases the value of those relationships in the form of real empathy and stronger support. That's Appreciation in a nutshell.

Those strategies have actually helped Appreciate *most* of my relationships. My initial instincts are now a little more finely tuned to recognize what other people might need. I've become a better listener and hopefully more receptive and reactive to the needs I see. As a husband, father, friend, son, colleague, boss, employee, or volunteer, I find myself calling on the same set of tools. And hopefully, I'm using them to achieve more positive outcomes, regardless of who is on the other side of the relationship.

As I think about each of these relationships that foster care has brought into our lives, it invites me to revisit one of my original and greatest hesitations about even getting involved in the first place. Remember that massive number? 400,000+ kids in the foster care system! As you'll recall, I approached that challenge fearful of its size and lacking confidence that I could make any real dent in it.

But of course, there was Carie, the constant voice of Godly assurance, whispering over the storm. What she encouraged me to consider was this. The battle isn't about solving the entire problem or even bringing that giant nationwide number down. You're in this to do whatever you can to make life better for those that God puts in your path – ONE life at a time. That shouldn't be just how we approach foster care. That's a powerful mantra for ALL relationships.

Sometimes, or even a lot of the time, it's hard. Sometimes you just get it wrong. Sometimes you doubt whether you're even helping. But frequently, as those young people came through our home, Carie would calm those fears, too. She would reinforce the value of what we were doing, reminding me that she took comfort in knowing something very basic. Even if a foster child didn't get 100% of our best during their time with us, she knew we were still *helping*. How? Every minute those children spent with us was a minute of their lives that NO ONE on earth needed to worry about whether they were cared for, safe, or loved.

Simply put, they were better off *with* us than they would have been without us. Put foster care aside, and imagine living all of your relationships through THAT lens! Pretty easy to appreciate.

I want to circle back once more to the definition of "relationship." In thinking about "how two or more people are connected," I realize that our experiences in foster care fundamentally changed how I process "relationships" in general. In addition to being cynical, I'm also fairly sentimental. I'm prone to holding onto things and getting emotionally invested. Typically, you might think this kind of attachment would be reserved for only the most important relationships. Depending on how you define "important," you might be right. Often, we think the importance of a relationship is a function of its duration. That is, the longer you've known someone, the more important they, and your relationship, becomes. Foster care has tweaked that dynamic for me. Why? Because at some point, I realized it isn't the DURATION of our relationships that dictates their importance – it is the DEPTH of what we are willing to give that creates the "connection."

I think God might feel the same way about His relationship with us. Consider one of the most quoted Scriptures ever.

John 3:16 - *"For God so loved the world that he gave his one and only Son, that whoever believes in him shall not perish but have eternal life."*

Our connection to Him is a direct function of what He gave for us. In terms of duration, He did this thousands of years before you or I even existed. What He was willing to give - His most precious gift; His own Son - demonstrates a depth of love which we can scarcely understand but can still try to appreciate.

Look at our definition again. "Relationship is *the degree to which* two things are connected." In a foster care situation, you find yourself giving your own most precious gifts (time, love, attention, support) to those kids. Sometimes it might even go beyond what you give your own children or your spouse. You become emotionally invested in a way that makes a "connection" inevitable - based on its depth and regardless of its length.

These "connections" are permanent in a way that mere "interactions" are not. For example, the foster kids we have cared for most often are a pair of sisters we saw every few weeks for more than a year. We developed real relationships with them – getting to know their personalities, likes, dislikes, quirks, senses of humor, etc. We were even blessed to attend the ceremony where their full-time foster parents adopted them. And we continue to have a relationship with that family to this day. That's a FOREVER connection. But, in their own ways, so are the connections we have with the kids we only saw for a day or so.

Again, Carie is the glue that holds all of this together. I think back to the second Christmas season after we started fostering. In the 18 or so months before then, we probably had about ten different individual foster children in our home – each of them a unique soul with whom we have memories and a connection. Carie had the beautiful idea to use a small Christmas tree we already had for a brand-new purpose. She and our boys crafted handmade ornaments that featured the names of every foster child who had been in our home to that point. Then, we had a special family ceremony that gave us a chance to focus on each of those children individually, recall memories of being with them, and pray for their current and future lives. Perhaps more so than any other time of the year, Christmas is a season of traditions. Whether we remain active in the foster system or not, I imagine that the building of and rejoicing over this little tree, and the lives it represents to us, is a tradition our family will probably honor forever. What a wonderful reminder of the permanency of "relationships," regardless of their length or proximity.

Attaching Appreciation to the Past

I've mentioned a little bit about how foster care has influenced my relationship with my children and how this is something I couldn't have seen or understood without the context of our experience. What's equally important, and probably wholly logical, but still slightly amazing to me, is how participating in foster care has informed my relationship with my *parents* as well.

As hopefully is evident from the stories I have already shared, my parents are fantastic human beings. They did a remarkable job with their children, especially given our circumstances. Like most of us, I didn't (know how to) appreciate the difficult, often thankless task of parenting until I had done it myself. Other chapters in this story speak in greater detail about the specific challenges my parents faced in raising both my sister and me. But I'll add here that they also did it all while starting a company, almost bankrupting it, and then using that experience to start another (which thrived for decades until their eventual retirement). I mention that because it informs a big part of my relationship with each of my parents.

My father was the "sales guy," constantly traveling and spending at least a couple of nights away from home most weeks of our childhood. My mother was the "office manager." She worked from home or nearby and was home either all the time or at least every night, probably no different than most families. In the context of my relationship with each of them, though, it's important. Earlier, I shared about being in and out of hospitals and having multiple surgeries as a child. In my unsophisticated child brain, I reduced that dynamic down to its simplest form: Mom is here (for me) all the time; Dad? I'm less sure about him. In hindsight, this is totally inaccurate and cruelly unfair. But it's a stark reminder of how our early experiences and thoughts drive so much of who we become, at least in our own heads.

Now, remember all that foster training I mentioned? Here it comes again to deliver more heartbreaking context and clarity. One of the expert sources we encountered in those sessions was Dr. Karyn Purvis. A renowned and respected developmental psychologist, Dr. Purvis was also a mother, grandmother, pastor's wife, teacher, and foster parent who became affectionately known as "The Child Whisperer" in pediatric psychology and foster care circles. In short, Karyn understood kids – particularly kids from hard places – in a way most others do not. Through her writings and video workshops, she would teach Carie and me many valuable strategies for communicating with, relating to, and disciplining children with a whole new level of effectiveness. As I've said previously, for the sake of the foster children we have served, our biological kids, and all of the youth I encounter in volunteering roles or life in general, I am immensely grateful for the knowledge we gained through her wisdom. But her teachings gave me an even greater gift – one that spans all of the generations in my life comprehensively.

In one of her video workshops, Dr. Purvis introduced us to the concept of "secure attachment." British psychologist John Bowlby pioneered Attachment Theory in the 1950s. In a nutshell, it suggests that our "attachments," or the emotional bonds we form with other humans, especially early on, set our expectations for security, comfort, and confidence in ways that can be lifelong. The central premise is that children develop a sense of security (or attachment) directly proportional to their primary caregivers' availability and responsiveness. More simply, kids who know their parents are "there for them" (physically, emotionally, spiritually, financially) usually become adults with a sense of "secure attachment." That correlates to high degrees of stability, adjustment, and confidence. Children who do not "attach" firmly are "insecure," which can lead to confusion, uncertainty, and lack of confidence in relationships in general. Worse, some are essentially "unattached." Kids whose formative relationships are negligent or abusive often suffer distrust, isolation, shame, guilt, anger, and a whole range of other negative emotions that impact how they see themselves and others. Sadly, many foster kids and other kids from hard places are shackled with these less-than-secure mentalities.

But Dr. Purvis offered a glimmer of hope. Even in kids who are almost entirely unattached, she suggests, it is possible – through constant and consistent positive reinforcement – to reprogram that mentality and actually heal the damage. Doing so while they are still children is far preferable and much easier than unpacking all of that damage in adults who have either dealt with it or not for years on end.

I studied psychology in college and have always been intrigued by how people think, act, and interact. At first, I simply found Dr. Purvis' presentation of the attachment concept "interesting." It wasn't until later, though, that I had an epiphany that would fundamentally change my understanding of relationships. At some point, I realized that my interpretation, and thus my view of my relationship with my own parents, was partially "unattached." I would never have articulated it that way, and even now, when I think about it, the term feels odd and inaccurate. But there is still some truth that in my childhood brain, I processed my mom as ever-present and my dad as much less so. I don't ever recall thinking of him as unreliable, and certainly never as negligent or abusive – just there less. In that way, I indeed formed a more attached relationship with my mom. Even through my early adult years, I found it much easier to connect with my mom than my dad. Thankfully though, with age has come some additional context, understanding, and yes, appreciation on my part of just how awesome BOTH of my parents were, and still are.

In hindsight, my perception of my dad's involvement and investment in my life was flawed, and unfairly so. And thankfully, whatever rifts there may have ever been between us were small and easily enough mended. I don't know if I would say that relationship was ever truly "broken." But even if it were, I'm confident it's ultimately "fixed" and attached at this point.

And yet, there was an even bigger epiphany still to come. If you've already read the chapter about our search for a church home, you'll know that I spent a lot of time feeling generally disconnected from God. I knew why, in pretty specific terms too, but until hearing from Dr. Purvis, I was missing the really big picture. Our union with God is supposed to be the ultimate parent-child relationship. We are supposed to be confident in His love for us and find His presence a source of constant comfort and strength. I had that until, through a series of dire circumstances, I looked around and couldn't see Him at work or even present in my life. In short, I realized that I had (either assumed or developed) an insecure attachment to God. Like those children from hard places, I was looking for a caregiver who was both available and attentive to my needs, and I didn't see one. In the absence of that comfort and security, I grew cynical – in faith, in relationships, and in general. Only now, years later, with the benefit of amazing relationships like the ones I have with Carie and my parents; the wisdom of teachers like Dr. Purvis; and the context of what others, like those kids from hard places experience; am I able to see it. Only now can I understand how and why that most important relationship became strained – and work in earnest to repair it.

What a blessing it is to be able to thank your parents for everything they are and have done – to show real appreciation for the love, support, time, and energy they've poured into your life. Becoming involved in foster care allowed me to see parent/child dynamics that were very different from my own. What a blessing it is to see, despite the challenges or circumstances I faced, just how fortunate I was to have two parents who loved, supported, and fought for me my entire life. And what a blessing it is to have that epiphany now - while my parents are still here to hear it, and I'm still actively raising my own kids. The literal Appreciation of that sequence is a greater focus on making sure my kids hopefully never feel that same sense of detachment when they think about our relationships.

And what a blessing it is to be reminded with such clarity the true nature of the parent/child dynamic of our relationship with God – the ever-present Heavenly Father who desires never to be unattached from his children. I'm still working on holding all those connections firmly together, but now, I do so with a completely renewed sense of appreciation.

As a sort of postscript to this particular chapter, I feel compelled to give a much deserved 'thank you' to another one of the inspired teachers we met along the way in our journey with the foster care ministry. Jason Johnson is a pastor from Texas, a foster parent, and a Director with the Christian Alliance for Orphans. Jason has written several books and travels extensively to speak to foster organizations and ministries. One night, in mid-2019, I happened to be sitting in a church sanctuary, earning some of those vital training hours, listening to Jason talk about his journey. I don't recall his exact words or even their specific context, but during his presentation, Jason used the word "appreciate" in a way that struck me oddly. As I've laid out here, "appreciate" has several unique definitions, and the way he used it that night was somehow not exactly intuitive. I also, unfortunately, don't recall what Jason said for a couple of minutes after that. Something flashed in my brain, and I started fixating on that one word. I thought about how what I took away from his story might be completely different than what he might have intended just because of the context of that one word. I couldn't get that word "appreciate" out of my head. I think it became a bit of a subconscious meditation for me – a planted seed that would ultimately spring to life when my son called me out for being a cynical pessimist. Had I not been there to hear Jason speak that night, that seed might never have been planted, and this series of essays – and any enlightenment they have brought me – might never have come to fruition. Thanks, Jason, sincerely. The gift of your words and your journey has had a giant impact on my own. I can and do Appreciate you.

Questions to Consider:

• What is an example of a problem SO big in your life you can't even imagine a solution?

• In what endeavors do you imagine yourself completely alone, without enough support to breakthrough and achieve a particular goal?

• Who around you might be in the same position, just needing SOMEONE to come alongside them and offer a little bit of life-changing help?

• What relationships in your life might benefit from a heightened sense of attention to what someone else needs?

Wisdom to Appreciate:

Proverbs 22:6 – "Start children off on the way they should go, and even when they are old they will not turn from it."

Philippians 2:5-7 – "In your relationships with one another, have the same mindset as Christ Jesus: Who, being in very nature[a] God, did not consider equality with God something to be used to his own advantage; rather, he made himself nothing by taking the very nature[b] of a servant."

1 John 3:1 – "See what great love the Father has lavished on us, that we should be called children of God! And that is what we are!"

John 3:16 – "For God so loved the world that he gave his one and only Son, that whoever believes in him shall not perish but have eternal life."

Chapter 8:
The Game of Life

I love baseball. This statement is true today and has been for at least a decade – but it was not always the case. For most of my nearly 50 years on this planet, I would say I was somewhat ambivalent about the sport. I can also honestly say there was a brief but specific time in my life when I definitely did NOT love or appreciate baseball.

A Rough First Outing

Earlier, I mentioned the pivotal role baseball played in my father's life. He was a stud pitcher, on scholarship at a Division I school, and on a legitimate path to playing professionally. Then, life threw him a curveball and instantly ended his baseball career. To say that baseball was, and still is, important to my dad is an understatement.

You may also recall the variety of physical challenges that are part of my story. So, it's easy to envision that when my dad's passion for baseball collided with my singular attempt during childhood to play the game he loved but had to abandon, the results were less than spectacular.

I'm not even sure it was me, but somewhere around the time I was 10 or 11, *someone* decided I should give baseball a try. My parents signed me up for a local league, and off I went. I was probably excited to try it, at least at first – although I don't have any specific memories of that. Nor could I tell you anything about how my Phillies did that season or even remember the name of a single other kid on that team. In fact, I only have TWO distinct memories of that one inglorious season. One involved my mom; the other, my dad.

My mom has always been my biggest cheerleader. She often reminded me that, despite my physical challenges, I also had other gifts that more than compensated. As it turns out, balance, coordination, speed, and physical strength contribute significantly to baseball success. I don't have any of those, but I still gave it a shot. Predictably, I spent most of my time buried in left field – me, and everyone else, praying the ball wasn't hit my way – and at the bottom of the batting order, almost a certain strikeout.

Somewhere near the middle of that season, after watching me come nowhere near getting on base, unless I walked, she had seen enough to know how things were going to go. So, my mom came up with a plan to motivate me towards finding some success. Cash. She straight up told me, "I'll give you $5 for every time you hit the ball." You read that right. She didn't say she would pay me to 'get a hit.' She was willing to fork over cash on the off chance that my bat merely struck a moving ball. As motivational plans go, it was kind of sad but sweet and very indicative of a mother's love for her struggling son. I think I may have fouled two balls off after that, netting myself a whopping $10.

My father, on the other hand, had a different perspective and a very different plan. Let me start by saying that I know there is a stereotypical trap of parents (usually dads) trying to live vicariously through their kids when it comes to sports. But here, at least in hindsight, I *almost* feel bad for my dad. He was still a young man, in his prime, and with the wounds of his own baseball journey's unceremonious end still fresh enough. I can only imagine how insanely frustrating it must have been for my dad to sit in the stands and watch me be objectively awful at one of the things he loved most in life. Sadly though, he could *want* me to be good at baseball with all his might. But it just wasn't gonna happen.

My dad wasn't just good at the physical act of playing baseball – he was and still is incredibly smart about the mental and tactical aspects of the game too. So, when he wanted to help me, I should have been able to trust and willingly follow his plan. There were a couple of problems with that, though. First, boys at that age don't always love hearing from their fathers that they're doing something wrong and need to make adjustments. We don't appreciate that. So again, my dad IS really smart about baseball. And he was right about why I wasn't good at hitting the ball. I was afraid of getting hit *by* the ball. But there was another problem, too. His proposed solution for that challenge was pretty unconventional.

One day, my dad took me to a field for a little extra practice. What started as pretty basic escalated quickly. My dad has a ton of admirable qualities. In the 35-year-old version of him, though, patience wasn't necessarily one of them. After reaching his limit for watching me fail to make adjustments with the bat, he decided to adjust his teaching technique. The result is responsible for my other lingering memory of baseball from childhood. His plan? Essentially, trial by fire. If the problem was me being afraid to swing the bat, his solution was to force the issue. His directions: "I'm gonna throw the ball. You're gonna swing. I don't care if the ball is in the dirt, or ten feet behind you, or straight at your head – you're gonna swing."

Wait, what? In my pre-teen head – the one he just mentioned throwing a baseball at – all I could think of was this grown man, formerly a Major League prospect, and currently struggling to control his temper, chucking baseballs at me. Terrifying? You bet. Motivating? Not really. And for good measure, he added: "Every time you don't swing, you're gonna run a lap."

Shockingly, that wasn't a fun experience, and you can guess how well it went. I'm pretty sure I ran more laps than I hit baseballs. I didn't exactly appreciate his "coaching" or even his parenting at that moment. But it is part of what I have come to

Appreciate about the larger story of which this small episode is part.

I finished that single, awful season of baseball and never played the game again on any organized level. It simply wasn't fun for me. I went on to experiment with other sports and discovered I really liked soccer. I was probably no better at that than I was at baseball, but it was a very different experience. For starters, I actually enjoyed playing the sport. Plus, there was no added pressure to be good at something in which someone *else* had an emotional investment. But perhaps the biggest reason for my joy was that I had an excellent coach. By that, I don't even mean that he was a brilliant soccer tactician – maybe he was, but we were kids, and I wouldn't have known it anyway. He made the game fun, balancing seriousness and play. He also understood what his players could and couldn't do and challenged them appropriately. That is something I could definitely Appreciate when the time came, and it would.

I share those stories about my early experiences with baseball only to illustrate how unlikely it was that I would wind up spending a considerable part of my own kids' childhoods very much involved in the game.

You've Got a Lot to Learn, Rookie

In the spring of 2010, our oldest son, Matt, was about to turn five. Like most kids that age, he was a ball of energy, and we were looking to get him involved in sports. As we drove through our community, we noticed a sign proclaiming that one of the local leagues would be offering FREE baseball that season. We had no idea if Matt would like, love, hate, or be utterly indifferent to baseball. But with literally nothing to lose, we went for it.

We had no idea what to expect when we showed up for registration and evaluations. It was pretty basic: lots of little kids running around while adults with clipboards watched, trying to rate their relative skills.

As a newcomer, it didn't occur to me just how much local youth sports leagues depend on volunteers. Those adults with the clipboards – they're the ones who will be the head coaches, but they're not just looking to draft players. They also need help from assistant coaches. Some of them already have those relationships and know that they will draft specific players to secure that kid's parent as an assistant. Others just wing it, draft a team, and then hit up all the parents until someone steps up to assist. I think Matt's first baseball coach fell squarely in this second category.

And so it was, based on little else but my desire to be involved with my son, that my one terrible season of baseball experience as a child landed me a role as an Assistant Coach for the 5U Mount Paran Grasshoppers tee-ball team.

Aside from how much fun Matt (and I) had, that first season, ten years ago, is a total blur now. It did, however, help Carie and I succeed in at least one aspect of parenting. All along, our goal for both our boys was to expose them to as many different outlets for their passion and creativity as possible and then support whatever stuck for them. Both of them would end up loving baseball, and each for unique reasons. But for Matt, in particular, that first season became an introduction to the game that would become one of the great passions of his young life. On that level alone, even if I never got involved, I could easily say I appreciated baseball for everything it gave just one of our kids. But the lessons were just getting started.

In those first few seasons, I learned that being an assistant coach, especially at the tee-ball level, isn't remarkably complicated. That's not to say that trying to coordinate 12 four- and five-year-olds (in baseball or any activity) is easy or stress-free. It's not. But at the end of the day, the stakes, and everyone's expectations, are pretty low. So, it's not like there was even an "I don't appreciate that" moment at the beginning of our baseball journey. But one was coming soon enough.

During Matt's first tee-ball season, Liam was only two and still a few years away from taking the field himself. That first season went well – for both of us, and when Matt decided to continue playing, I also chose to stay involved. Each new season, I would volunteer to help as an assistant, growing my knowledge of the game, happily spending quality time with my oldest son, and developing new relationships along the way. A few seasons later, once Liam jumped into the action, things moved to a whole other level.

Remember those pre-season evaluations and drafts? Every season, that same process plays out like clockwork. Except, what happens when there are more teams than coaches? I was about to find out. Our boys are just under two years apart in age. So roughly half the time, they played in the same age group. In Liam's second season, they would be playing on the same team – which is great for several reasons, except one.

Usually, following evaluations, you just wait for an email from one of the coaches letting you know that your kid is on a specific team and when to show up for practice. That's what I was expecting. What I got was a phone call. The league's commissioner called to let me know they had completed the draft, and there was one team with no head coach – my boys' team. That was the *bad* news. The *good* news was that one of the other coaches – a guy I had assisted previously – had told everyone, "I know a guy who would be a great coach. Just call him and tell him we drafted a team for him, with his kids on it, and they need a coach; he'll do it." Guess my response. The endorsement aside, I didn't really appreciate that at all.

I'm pretty sure I tried to say no. I offered to help as an assistant, but I really didn't want the job of head coach. The commissioner suggested another dad on this team felt the same way, and perhaps we could share the responsibility. That sounded better, but I still wasn't sure. I'd learned a lot in those first few seasons, but I still didn't feel like I knew very much. Moreso, though, I didn't love the idea of my very shallow expertise being responsible for the baseball success (or failure) of a group of 6-year-olds. After some hemming and hawing, and a call or two with that other dad, he convinced me that if I took the role of head coach, he would do everything he could to support me and that together we would figure it out. I accepted and very reluctantly began my career as a little league head baseball coach.

I would never have gone looking for that opportunity on my own. I would have been happy to continue being a helper without taking another step up to actually lead. You may have noticed a pattern forming here. It's something I refer to as the "Batman and Robin" dynamic. Essentially, some people desire and are built for top billing. They like or even crave being front and center, or the "hero." Others are more comfortable being the trusted sidekick, doing meaningful work that contributes to success, but living a step or two outside the spotlight. From school projects to career roles, committees, and other endeavors, I've almost always preferred to be Robin vs. Batman, and coaching baseball was no different.

I'm self-aware and honest enough to admit that I prefer "Robin" roles. In the few times I chose or was chosen to be Batman, it worked out fine. I *am* capable of stepping up and succeeding. But I think I'm probably a situational Batman at best.

Don't get me wrong. I know that the nature of growth (physically, mentally, and spiritually) is that at first, it hurts, and then it feels good. As some of these stories demonstrate, many of my most rewarding moments have come from stepping outside my comfort zone. And, I have to remind myself, some of the most amazing things in my life are only here because I made that stretch. My choice to be a Batman on the baseball field is a prime example. The many blessings and lessons I got from that decision are remarkable, and among those I appreciate most even today.

Maybe the most ironic thing about the path that brought me to coaching was one of the first guides I had on that road. That other coach, the one I had helped before, who in turn helped me right under the bus and into a head coaching role? His name is Stephen, too, and he's actually a great guy and still a good friend this many years later. And it turns out I would end up owing him one of the biggest debts of gratitude of anyone I've ever known. I don't even know if he genuinely thought I would be good at the task for which he blindly volunteered me. I might just have been a name he came up with when they went around the room, asking who they could get to coach that extra team. In the end, it doesn't matter. What really matters is the realization of everything I would have missed if I had stuck to my selfish guns and said no to that first opportunity outside of my comfort zone.

I mentioned what a great guy Stephen is. I truly enjoyed being his assistant, not least because his teams almost always won. That's fun when you're on the same side, but not nearly as much fun from the other dugout. As much as I enjoyed coaching *with* Stephen, I really didn't appreciate the challenge of coaching *against* him. In fact, he became one of a few guys in that league I might even have considered a rival – the guy you desperately wanted to beat, mostly because usually, you didn't.

It fits then that in the last season he coached before moving away to another state, our teams would meet in an elimination game in the league tournament's semi-final. For whatever reason, God and good fortune smiled on my little squad that day, and I somehow managed to notch what was probably only my second or third win ever (in many tries) against one of his teams. Stephen, of course, was gracious and congratulatory afterward. It wasn't lost on me though – before, during, or after – that this would likely be the last time he and I would ever see each other as opposing coaches on a baseball field. Afterward, once we'd both done our post-game talk with our players and parents, I ran into Stephen in the parking lot. I'm sure I was still riding a wave of joy from the victory itself, but there was something else there stirring my emotions, too. I was overcome with gratitude. I approached him, offered my hand, and when he shook it, I found myself pulling him in for a 'bro-hug.' I thanked him sincerely for throwing me under the coaching bus and explained that in doing so, he had given me one of the greatest gifts I had ever received. It was already true then, but I had no idea how much longer that list of blessings would become.

"It's Cool, Dad. I Don't Need You."

Among the greatest of those gifts was an evolution in the relationship I have with my sons. Like all children, our two boys are uniquely wonderful creations. Though similar in some ways, they are also vastly different – in temperament, motivation, and expression. Matt is an archetypal first-born: independent, self-driven, focused, and often clear of course. Liam is a classic younger sibling: creative, outgoing in specific areas of interest, flexible, and a little closer to the nest.

So, after a few seasons of baseball, it came as little surprise that each of them would begin to look at and approach the game differently. I mentioned that our boys were roughly two years apart. This span meant that MOST of the time, they would be in the same league. In the third season of them both playing, the opposite was true, and it created a crossroads. There are plenty of parents out there ready, willing, and able to juggle the coaching responsibilities of not just one, but two or even three teams if it means getting to stay with their own kids. I figured I could manage to help or coach one team, but I knew coaching two just wasn't in the cards from a time and physicality standpoint.

By the time Matt was nine and Liam was seven, I had a decision to make. I thought it would be an issue. I imagined both boys vying equally for me to stay with them and their team and figured we were heading for a compromise or conflict. I was wrong, and once again, it was my oldest son who showed the way forward. Somewhat matter-of-factly, Matt said something like: "It's cool, Dad. I don't need you." That was a pretty confident statement for a nine-year-old and a bit of a double-edged sword for a parent of any age.

On the one hand, he's asserting himself and showing independence and security. You have to love that. On the other hand, he literally said he didn't need me (to coach him) anymore. Of course, his statement was singularly specific to that one activity, and he wasn't discarding me permanently before even reaching double digits, but it was kind of heartbreaking nonetheless. His declaration did provide a solution to the immediate challenge, though, which was good. It also helped reveal something far more valuable.

Perhaps you've heard of the concept of "love languages." In the early 1990s, marriage and relationship counselor Dr. Gary Chapman published a groundbreaking work called *The 5 Love Languages®*. The basic premise is that as unique people, each with different personalities, we all understand, express, and receive love differently. Dr. Chapman called these specific communication pathways the "5 Love Languages." They are Words of Affirmation, Acts of Service, Receiving Gifts, Quality Time, and Physical Touch. Each of us tends to respond more intensely and effectively to some of these inputs than others. They are not mutually exclusive. We might react to any or all of them in various situations or relationships, but we all have at least one of these languages in which we prefer primarily to give and receive. Understanding the Love Language of someone with whom you are trying to have any kind of meaningful, productive relationship can make a huge difference.

The concept of Love Languages is one I would first encounter as part of a marriage and relationships workshop Carie and I attended at our church. It would also reappear and be crucially valuable in our ongoing training around foster care. But what does that have to do with coaching little league baseball? Quite a lot.

Matt's primary love language is Words of Affirmation. He is a high-striver who often succeeds, but also craves, and thrives from, encouragement along the way. When Matt told me he didn't need me on the baseball field anymore, he was essentially saying he was ready to fly on his own a little bit. He didn't even need a push out of the nest – only for me to tell him it would be fine when he jumped on his own. He just needed to hear I knew he would do great and have fun whether I was right there beside him or not.

Our youngest, Liam, speaks with, hears, and responds to a different voice altogether. While Words of Affirmation are also important to him, his primary love language is Quality Time. He has always been the one who wants to stay close – to cuddle up on the couch and watch a movie, or engage you in playing a game, or just hang out together in the same room. Matt prefers a little bit of space; Liam wants to be right next to you. Without them even knowing it, those truths were precisely what they were communicating in answering the question of their coaching preferences. I wasn't even fully familiar with the concept of love languages during this specific conversation with them. But in hindsight, it's clear these languages develop early, and our boys were already fluent. And I can tell you, they remain constant over time.

So, I let one child go his own way and embrace his self-confidence while I held the other close. Whether they or even I knew it at the time, this is what their hearts were requesting through their unique love languages. In this instance, baseball was simply the vehicle that presented the lesson that helped me recognize a greater truth about human relationships in general – a lesson worth applying and Appreciating as often as possible.

Love languages are a great example of how each of us is unique. Again, look at Psalm 139:14.

David writes: *"I praise you because I am fearfully and wonderfully made; your works are wonderful, I know that full well."*

Here, he's reminding us that God's masterful plan all along is to endow us all with unique attributes and talents.

Youth sports turns out to be a great example – even among 7- and 8-year-old baseball players. Step onto a field with a group of them, or even just watch closely from the stands, and you'll quickly see that they're all built differently. Within any given two-year age group (whether it's 5-6 or 15-16), the difference between the youngest/smallest kid and the oldest/biggest kid is usually significant, visually and physically. They all also have different skills and relative strengths and weaknesses. That's precisely why tryouts precede every season and why those evaluations attempt to measure various abilities. The shortest kid might not be the strongest, but he might be the fastest. The biggest kid might be the slowest, but he can probably hit or throw the ball farther. Ideally, the best teams – in endeavors athletic or otherwise – are a collection of complementary skills. When combined correctly by a smart leader, those skills provide balance and comprehensively cover the teams' needs. That, among other things, is the coach's job. Evaluate your team, decipher their unique strengths, and then put them in positions that maximize their unique talents in a way that leads to collective success.

So, what happens when your team members are 7-year-olds with no idea what some of their talents are because they've not yet had a chance to discover them? Potentially, it's something extraordinary and even life-changing.

Hidden Talents & Secret Weapons

In my fourth or fifth season of coaching, through a combination of luck and my own shortcomings as a talent evaluator, I ended up with what can be best described as an "unbalanced" team of 7- and 8-year-old players. Sometimes you end up drafting kids who don't even show up for evaluations, so you take a flyer and hope for the best. They could turn out to be hidden gems that catapult your team to the top, or not. Like all the other teams that season, mine had a couple of "studs," a couple of "rookies" who had never played before, and then several kids somewhere in the middle. In total, though, my team was heavy on small kids who were neither particularly small, fast nor coordinated. After just a few practices, I realized we might need to get a little creative if we were going to succeed. We still practiced all the fundamentals, of course (catching, throwing, fielding, hitting, and running), but there was one kid in particular who opened my eyes to a completely different opportunity and taught me another great lesson.

This player was one of the smallest on the team. He had played a season or two already and was thoroughly engaged, which for that age group is at least half of a coach's challenge. He was well coordinated but not very strong. So, while he could field the ball exceptionally well, he couldn't throw it very far. Luckily for him and us, the second base position is custom made for a player like that. Just about anything that came his way, he could get to, scoop up, and either run or throw to first or second base to help us get an out. I always told my players that it was their job to find at least ONE way to help their team. If every player did that, the collective effort usually resulted in success. That reminder also helps temper the constant frustration of playing baseball, which cruelly, is a game filled with opportunities to fail.

From a pretty early age, baseball coaches try to get young players to understand this truth, telling them things like "even the best hitters in history only batted around .300 for their careers." Think about that. The Baseball Hall of Fame is FULL of guys who "failed" at their jobs 65-70% of the time. I don't know if that makes 7-year-olds who can't hit very well feel better, but this almost 50-year-old appreciates the reminder that success and perfection aren't even remotely the same thing.

Anyway, this particular player, Ethan, had already found one way to help his team. Defensively he was an asset at a crucial position. Sadly though, he couldn't see what he was doing well because he was too busy focusing on what he didn't like or thought wasn't "good enough." How often are we all guilty of the same self-sabotage?

Ethan wanted to be a good hitter. And, it's not even that he wasn't. He had good eye-hand coordination, which is priceless when it comes to hitting a moving baseball. Ethan's challenge was his stature and relative strength. He had just enough power to ensure that any ball he hit would go about as far as one of the bases, where a defensive player stood waiting to snare it and convert it for an easy out. He had a high rate of contact, but a low on-base percentage. That's a classic example of success being seen as failure, depending entirely on your perspective.

One day, early in that season, we were in the batting cages, doing a little hitting work. Ethan stepped into the batter's box and stood ready to hit. I think he might have been borrowing a teammate's bat, one even heavier than his own. He could barely swing it around in time to catch up to the balls I was lobbing in for him. I told him to move his hands up the barrel a little to make the hitting end shorter and lighter. He probably didn't fully understand my instructions or the intent, but the result – happy mistake that it might have been – was miraculous. His hands were so far up on the handle that he was almost swinging half a bat. As a result, he couldn't really take a full swing. The high hands and shortened arc, coupled with his excellent eye-hand coordination, created solid contact but very little distance. It also created an unexpected connection in my head. I was essentially watching a 7-year-old BUNT. That happy accident gave me an idea I couldn't wait to try.

During our next field practice, I changed my original plan and introduced the whole team to the concept of bunting – a skill rarely seen in 7-8 coach-pitch baseball. As always, we explained the idea, and the mechanics and then did drills that allowed each kid to practice the new skill. Finally, we created a competition among the players to see who could execute it with the most precision and consistency. You won't be surprised at the results. Several kids could actually perform the basic skill of bunting. But, most of those were our best "power" hitters, players who you would never ask to bunt in a game, and frankly, who wouldn't want to. Among the less proficient hitters, there was, perhaps predictably, less success. Then, there was Ethan. That little kid had the perfect combination of eye-hand coordination and "touch" to land a ball about six feet down the third (or even first) baseline, perfectly placed between infielders. And, he was plenty fast enough to beat even an accurate throw (which was never a certainty at that age) to first base.

In that very first bunting practice, Ethan probably placed 80% of his attempts with near perfection. That's very good – for him and his team, but it's not even close to the best part of the story. After he decimated his teammates in the bunting competition, as we moved on to another drill, Ethan came bounding toward me, his face beaming. I noticed his smile, and I congratulated him on his success. His response was one simple sentence that has stuck with me for the past five years and probably will for the rest of my life. Through that giant smile, he said: "Wow! I didn't know I could do that."

I'm sure I probably said something like, "Dude, you're awesome," and I was certainly happy for him. But it didn't register for me until later what had truly happened. In a single moment, that child went from seeing himself as deficient in something he wanted to improve, to being a champion of a new skill he didn't even know existed a few days earlier. And, he could Appreciate that.

Have you've ever been lucky enough to have a front-row seat for when someone discovered a new talent – let alone one you may have had even the smallest hand in helping them uncover? Let me tell you, for a coach, and maybe even just as a human, it might not ever get better than that.

Ethan was so proficient at this new skill that we decided to try it for real in our next game. We even created a special "sign" for Ethan when he came up to bat, letting him know it was time to bunt. Because it was coach-pitch, I (depending on my accuracy that day) had the opportunity to serve up pitches to my batters exactly where I knew they could hit them. In that very next game, Ethan came up to bat with two outs and teammates on first and second base. Historically, it was incredibly likely he would hit a ground ball to an infielder, ending the inning. Instead, as Ethan stepped into the batter's box, I slyly gave him our new bunt sign. I was standing about fifteen feet away, but I could still see the smile form on his face as he nodded, confirming the plan. I lobbed the ball. Ethan squared around like a seasoned pro and dropped a beautiful bunt a quarter of the way down the third baseline. The catcher and third baseman both froze, presumably never having seen a bunt in a live game before. The pitcher, after a significant delay, broke for the ball. He fielded it and did the thing he was trained to do, throw to first. But the oddity of the play, and length of the throw, made that more difficult. His throw was wild, getting past the first baseman and into shallow right field. Ethan was safe at first. The runners advanced, one scoring and the other landing on third. With one quarter-swing of the bat, little Ethan made a huge impact, dropping a perfectly executed 10-foot RBI single that helped us win that game. His reaction was priceless, but so was that of the opposing coaches and even the people in the stands. Mostly, they wanted to know, "did you just see that?" or "did he *mean* to do that?" I *did* see it, and he *did* mean it. It was glorious.

The impact of Ethan's new skill would echo for the rest of that season. After that, he assumed the nickname of "Buntmaster," which always made him, and me, smile. Even better, as the season progressed, he had many more opportunities to test his new skill. The first few times, it was a secret weapon of sorts that caught everyone by surprise. By about the third game, it had become known throughout the league. At a certain point, each time Ethan stepped up to bat, you would hear opposing coaches yell, "watch the bunt!" at their defenses. Some of them were even spending time in practices now teaching their own teams how to execute and defend bunts. By the end of the season, defenses had flattened the curve to the point that it wasn't always successful. Now, sometimes when he bunted, Ethan got out. But the result was almost always net gain because we also used it as a sacrifice technique to advance runners into scoring position.

In that context, as coaches, we were also able to use it as a lesson for our players about the larger concept of "sacrifice," where one person gives up something that they value (in this case, a successful at-bat) for the good of others. Again, these kids were 7- and 8-year-olds, so some of that goes over their heads, but some of it doesn't.

As I feared from the outset, based on our team's make-up, we didn't win a ton of games that season. But we did help one kid turn a perceived negative into a very real positive and introduce an entire team to a concept like self-sacrificial service to others in the process. I'll take those as wins any day.

Also, there truly is no better feeling than the deep sense of joy that comes from sharing an "I didn't know I could do that" moment with another person. I'll keep looking for opportunities to Appreciate that too.

Have Mercy. Give Grace.

Sacrifice is a valuable construct. I'm glad my kids and many of the players I have coached over the years have had the opportunity to encounter and practice it through sports. But it's just one of the several crucial life concepts baseball has helped illuminate for me. Another is mercy, which is essential in its own right, but made all the more powerful when placed in the context of another (potentially even more valuable) concept – grace.

If you're familiar at all with competitive sports, especially at the youth level, you've encountered the "Mercy Rule." In a nutshell, this allows a game to end before it's full completion if one team is so far ahead of the other that it is all but impossible for the trailing team to catch up. Sometimes two teams meet that are so far apart in ability that the score gets very lopsided. In leagues for the youngest of baseball players, there are rules limiting the number of runs one team can score in any inning. In theory, this keeps the total score relatively close throughout. At a certain point, though, that rule goes away. And baseball is unique in that the shift between offense and defense is dictated purely by the defense's ability to record three outs against the offense and not by any clock. For a team struggling to stop its opponent's offensive attack, there could be potentially no end to the onslaught.

I've been on both sides of this dynamic, as a coach and a spectating parent. I can tell you that while it can be great fun to watch your own kid's team jump out to a big lead, it can also kind of suck to be on either side of a total blowout. When you look up and see the score is 13-0 and it's only the second inning, it can stop being "fun" pretty quickly. Almost everyone involved is ready to move on, and you legitimately start praying for a merciful end to the suffering. Usually, after three of four innings of such imbalance, the officials step in and call the game. That's the Mercy Rule. Essentially, the "judges" decide that everyone involved has "had enough." The winners have proven their dominance, and the losers have had more than enough misery.

Some will say things like "mercy is for the weak," or that teaching such a concept makes people, and especially kids, "soft." Author George Eliot (Mary Ann Evans) once famously wrote: "We hand folks over to God's mercy, and show none ourselves." Sadly, that can be a common stance in our world. I suppose, in rare instances, where your life is in legitimate danger, approaching your adversary with no mercy might be understandable. For most, though, the vast majority of us unlikely to ever face mortal combat in real life; mercy is a choice. So what does God's Word say about it?

In Luke 6:36, we get, *"Be merciful, even as your Father is merciful."* This, of course, refers to God the Father, but it applies to our Earthly relationships, too. Matthew 5:7 tells us, *"Blessed are the merciful, for they shall receive mercy."* This is both a basic restatement of the Golden Rule to "treat others as you would have others treat you" and an excellent karmic reminder that whether we believe it or not, we usually reap what we sow.

I started off talking about baseball. Then, in joining the concepts of mercy and grace, seemingly wandered off on a tangent. Stick with me. Those two roads are about to converge again.

"Mercy" is often defined as "compassion or forgiveness shown toward someone you have the power to punish or harm." More simply, "mercy" is "when you DON'T get what you (may) deserve." Now, let's talk about grace. "Grace," put as simply, is "when you get what you DON'T deserve." It's sort of like the benefit of the doubt, but on a whole different level, especially when we're talking about God's Grace. But what does that have to do with baseball? I'll tell you.

A few years ago, my youngest son's team played in the semifinals of a summer all-star district tournament. On the line was a berth in the state tournament, a huge accomplishment. Fatefully, our opponents were a team from basically our backyard. Ours was a church league team, viewed by many as a "hurray for everyone" organization where competitive dominance might not have been the highest priority. The neighboring league – our opponent that day – was where many "high-caliber" players who left our park looking for a bigger challenge often landed. Because of the two parks' proximity, many of the families from both sides were familiar with each other. A lot of these kids had played ball and gone to school together for years. Had we not been playing head-to-head, we probably would each be rooting for each other to win. But not that day.

Before the game, several kids on each side came together to say hey, high-five, and maybe even talk a little good-natured smack. Everyone was looking forward to a fun game between friendly rivals. It didn't take long for things to go sideways. From the very beginning, there was confusion and drama. On the first pitch of the game, their lead-off hitter swung and looped a ball into right field for what turned out to be a double. But something was off. A regulation baseball makes a very distinct sound coming off a standard metal bat. Instead, this noise was totally different – muffled as if the ball was wrapped in a blanket. One of the game balls provided to the umpires by the coaches was a "soft" practice ball. It had a spongy rubber core instead of hardened cork as regulation game balls should be. It was a fluke, but one that resulted in a distinct advantage to the hitter, as that ball went much further than it normally would have. The sound it created also caused immediate confusion, and hesitancy, in our players. As coaches, we requested that since this was the first pitch of the game, it be nullified, and we start again. The umpires quickly refused that request, chalking it up to "bad luck." That bad luck got worse for us when that lead runner, who might otherwise not even have been on base, scored his team's only run that inning. No need for grace, yet.

The game progressed, and our rivals stretched their lead a bit more. As the batting order turned over and their kids came up to bat a second time, more drama ensued. The other team appeared to have batted out of order. If noted, this infraction is supposed to result in an automatic out. We didn't realize it at the time, but they fielded two kids wearing the same uniform number that day, which created extra confusion. Between innings, the coaches and umpires talked. That conversation, which included a study of the official lineups submitted before the game, revealed two new pieces of information.

First, our opponents had actually batted out of order a total of TWICE so far that game. But their roster had another issue too. These summer all-star tournaments were supposed to be exclusively for kids who had played in that park's preceding spring season. We had played our cross-town rivals more than once that summer and were pretty familiar with them, on and off the field. So, when that day's roster contained a couple of players we had never seen before, including one of their best performers, we were a bit curious. Each of these situations (the multiple lineup infractions and the potential improper participation) were individually sufficient for us to demand a forfeit of the game – a result that would send our little church team to the state tournament and send our rivals home in shame.

The officials paused the game for several minutes. Confusion grew among players and parents as the coaches and umpires consulted each other and the rule book. Eventually, they called the district tournament director to the field to help decide how to proceed. He reiterated that our team had the right to request a formal forfeit. This complicated process would involve more study of the batting order and scorebook and an investigation of all of their players' birth certificates and registration to ensure eligibility. Here is where I have to admit my own embarrassing shortcomings. I was an assistant coach on this team and involved in the discussions up to this point. I was also a father of a player on the field (and another kid in the stands). And, I was the former coach of almost every player on our team, and a few of those on the other side too. I had an emotional investment in a LOT of those kids, but I also wanted what *I* wanted. Instinctively, what I wanted was justice. It seemed like the other team – intentionally or not – had not followed the rules, and as such, there should be consequences. My default was pressing for a forfeit. But it wasn't my decision. That fell to our head coach, who thankfully happened to be the exact right person in precisely the right spot at the ideal time. His name is Eric, and aside from being among my dear friends for over a decade now, he is also one of the finest human beings I know.

As a church league, you might expect that just about every coach in our organization would be a shining example of admirable, Godly qualities. For the most part, that was true. All of us, myself included, had our less than stellar moments, though. But as is the case with any company, league, or organization, people earn different levels of esteem. When it comes to teaching and modeling righteous, honest, and admirable behavior, Eric occupies a place on my personal Mt. Rushmore. So, while I might have been incapable of making such a decision, especially in the heat of that moment, Eric reached a remarkably graceful conclusion.

The tournament director turned to him and said, "So, what do you want to do, Coach?" Eric looked at the scoreboard – we were losing by a few runs, with just a couple more innings to play. He looked at our kids, and then the others, many of whom he knew and had also coached. Then he said something I've taken with me since that day. "I don't want us to win or them to lose that way. Let it go. Let's play." I was a little surprised; not that Eric would make such a decision, but just in general. I had been leaning the other way and was prepared to celebrate an ill-gotten win before he righted the ship. The teams returned to their dugouts and prepared to resume play, the contention officially settled. You won't be surprised by the outcome – at least on the field.

We lost that game. There had been enough discussion during the break that everyone involved knew the basic plotline, including our players. These were 9- and 10-year-old kids, who had just lost a chance to go to State, to their friendly rivals, under questionable circumstances. A sense of injustice was strong in the dugout as we packed up our gear for what we thought might be the last time that season. We gathered in the stands for a post-game talk, which included a full explanation to both the players and parents of what had happened, and more importantly, why we (Eric, really) came to the decision we had. Perhaps not coincidentally, our own church (different from the one that hosted our team's league) had recently discussed the concepts of mercy and grace. Our pastor had conveniently furnished me with those simple definitions I shared with you a few moments ago. "Mercy" is NOT getting what you do deserve. "Grace" is getting what you do NOT deserve. So simple, even a (mad, frustrated) child could understand.

At that moment, I was so grateful for that wisdom. After Eric finished his remarks, he asked us assistants if we had anything to add. We congratulated our boys on playing hard and well, and then I shared those definitions with the team. Our rivals might have been the better team, and they might have beaten us anyway. But given how it all went down, we (again, ultimately Eric) ended up with a difficult decision to make. They had all seen the Mercy Rule in effect before. And here, our opponents probably did NOT get what they rightfully deserved in that situation, so there was definitely some mercy in play. But, along with it, at least in equal measure – grace. In allowing the game to continue uncontested, Eric had essentially relinquished the power to punish someone and instead bestowed upon them something they might not deserve.

Welcome to the Grace Rule – an excellent standard for how we should strive to treat each other in any situation where we feel slighted. Why? Because it's how God treats each of us – with Grace – forgiving with love and mercy as we continuously fall short of His glory. In Matthew 5:39, we get the well-known directive to "turn the other cheek." This is not to suggest that we should constantly roll over and let others treat us unfairly or unkindly. But, how much closer to His glory could we all be if the Grace Rule became a standard response to our perceived slights? We also shouldn't abandon the quest for true justice when needed, but, affording others grace, or at least being slower to judge their motives and actions, does bring us closer to understanding each other and God.

On our young players' faces, tears and frustration slowly gave way to understanding, empathy, and pride. And let's talk about pride for a second. The other thing I shared with those boys that day was how proud they should be – certainly for how they played the actual game between the lines, but for so much more. Whether they knew it or not, they should be proud to represent an organization that creates adults and kids with the strength to live out its values of "competition without compromise," especially when given an easier choice not to. I closed by telling them something I really needed to remember myself. They were 10-year-olds. There would be plenty more baseball in their futures. Still, they needed to remember that day. Because no matter how much longer they played or how many future coaches they had, never in their entire lives would they play for a man with as much integrity as Eric demonstrated that day. I got a little choked up telling them that, and those feelings return as I write this years later. That's a good thing. It means it resonates and matters. Winning is great, and it does matter, in the sense of having goals and achievements to justify all the hard work you invest in your endeavors. But HOW you win, and even how you lose, matters more. That's true on the little league field, in classrooms and boardrooms, in the political arena, and every other place you'll be tested in this life.

Even better, and this is something I've come to appreciate more and more over time, is the amazing gratification that comes from being able to honestly tell a child that their parent is "a good person." Eric's son is one of Liam's best friends and a child I love as if he were my own. He was on that team, too, and he was listening as we talked. Looking a 10-year-old in the face and telling him his dad is a good man might make you (and them) want to cry. But those would be tears of joy and pride, and those feel kind of good.

I saw those 10-year-olds' faces when I pointed out the goodness of their leader. They were proud of him, and in some way of themselves for being under his watch. What a gift it is to assure children that they're in the charge of good and worthy people. The comfort and pride that comes with that knowledge are akin to what we feel when we realize that we, as children of God, are in the constant stead of His goodness.

It might seem weird; publicly acknowledging that someone is a "good person" sounds like the kind of sentiment often saved for funerals. Don't wait for that. Tell kids, and adults too, as often as it's true and warranted that their leaders are good people. It might not feel like it at the moment, but that's better than a trip to State any day.

The Power of Reputation

That last story is just one example of the power of integrity in leadership. By choosing for our sons to play their formative years of baseball in this particular church league, we (and they) were fortunate to see such behavior modeled consistently by a cast of many remarkable coaches. In fact, a year or so earlier, Matt's team faced a similar test.

The stage and stakes were nearly identical – a playoff game against a known local rival, with a chance to advance to the State tournament on the line. The cast of characters, however, was quite different. Matt's opponents were also one of the local powerhouse teams, one with a reputation as "hard to beat" and maybe just as hard to like. Our all-star teams had played theirs often in tournaments. Those games were competitive, but usually, we came up short.

You'll sometimes hear coaches talk about having "special" teams – ones that, for one reason or another, stick out among all the others. Matt's team that season probably qualified as special. They were solid athletically, but more so, there was something about the chemistry of that team that was unique. Looking back now and seeing who the coaches and players were, I recognize what it was. The quality of character on that team, in terms of maturity and leadership, was exceptional. It's said that teams take on the personality of their coaches, and this happened, too. That team was led by several men whose knowledge of baseball was surpassed only by their passion for people and love of God. That's a powerful combination, especially when it comes to modeling reputable behavior and molding young people.

But I digress. Back to the field. This particular game of Matt's also started with an air of confusion, and for a similar reason. Again, these all-star tournaments were *supposed* to feature kids playing in their leagues' previous recreational seasons. Ours, for example, held a tryout each spring. At its conclusion, coaches chose 11 or 12 players for the summer all-star team, which is pretty straightforward. That was the team – no additions or subtractions thereafter. Not everyone took the same approach.

As I mentioned, we were familiar with our rivals that day. In fact, we had just played the "same" team a few short weeks ago in another tournament. We had even eked out a rare, close win against them, so it was memorable. Oddly though, as the teams arrived for this game, the same uniforms showed up, but several new kids wore them. A quarter of their roster that day were kids we had never seen before. That kind of thing gets noticed and talked about - a lot - in the stands as the game goes on. Through various conversations, we pieced together that apparently, this organization had more than one summer team and that they had "scrambled" them to form one "super" team for their run to State. Depending on your view, that might not be "breaking" the rules, but it does walk right up to the line and blur it a little bit. I guess maybe a different way to put it is that the tactic employed by this team in the name of winning was something our coaches would never have even considered. It just didn't seem right.

The game went on. As usual, it was close. To perhaps everyone's surprise, our little team clung to the smallest of leads going into the last inning. We were holding our own and maybe even playing a little bit above our heads. Whispers and prayers started running through the stands about a chance to go to State. We just had to hold them off for one more frame. Except, we didn't. They came back – first to tie, and then to pull ahead, in their last at-bat. As the home team, we would have one more chance. With the tying run on base and two outs, we watched with bated breath as one of the coach's sons – an excellent contact hitter with good speed – stepped in. He battled well, fouling off a couple of tough pitches and working himself to a full count. One more ball, and we would have the winning run aboard. The next pitch found the outside corner, and the umpire rang him up for a strikeout, looking to end the game – and our season. The image of that kid collapsing in the batter's box in despair is still etched in my brain.

As parents, we prepared to console our heartbroken players. Because it was a regional semifinal, fans from other teams were there, too. As we left the field and walked through the crowd, we heard sentiments like "well, THAT was the real championship game" and "those were the two best teams left." The other semifinal featured two teams who had enjoyed less than stellar seasons. Apparently, the local "experts" gave the winner of that game no chance to beat the team we had just played. They were right. The next night, our rivals coasted to State, and our season was over – or so we thought.

The State tournament is an invitational event. You win your region; you get invited. A certain number of teams are needed to fill that bracket, and sometimes, life just happens. Apparently, life "happened" to at least one of those qualifying teams, and they had to withdraw. That triggers a search for a replacement, where regional directors consult on worthy candidates. Our season ended on a Friday night. On Sunday evening, we got a call from Matt's coach, asking if we had plans for the following weekend. We said, "Well, no, now that baseball is over, we don't." His reply? "Baseball might not be over."

I couldn't believe what he said next. Our team had received an invitation to play at State based on our showing in the regional tournament. That call came at around 9:00 PM. Matt had already gone to bed, but I couldn't wait until morning to tell him. We woke him up from a dead sleep to share this fantastic news. You know that face kids make when they walk downstairs on Christmas morning and finally see all the presents Santa left – the ones they'd been dreaming about for months? Based on his reaction, including legit tears of joy, Christmas came in July that year. Seeing your child that excited, particularly about something unexpected and literally beyond their wildest expectation? That's pretty special.

That's a long story, especially not to even get to the point I wanted to make about integrity. But that's because it's not the end of the story. Matt's team would go on to play at the State tournament that next weekend. All eleven kids and their families were thrilled. It was a little bit like we were playing with house money, considering it a "win" just to be there. Essentially, it was grace that had brought us. We hadn't won our way there; in which sense we got something we didn't deserve. Our job then? Appreciate the opportunity to the best of our ability. Here's how that played out.

From the start, we knew our kids had an uphill battle. Almost every other team there was a regional champion, so the competition was stout. They would probably be lucky to win a game. They didn't.

But they *did* play the game the same way they always had – with respect, reverence, and joy. And, just as they had after every other game of their young lives – years at this point – they invited their rivals to join them in circling the mound for a moment of prayer. As a coach in that league myself, I know a few things about those prayers. Usually, they are prayers of thanksgiving – a moment of gratitude to God for the blessings that brought us all together, for keeping us safe as we played, for the opportunity to compete in the spirit of teamwork and good sportsmanship, and to be great examples of His love, on and off the field. The other thing I know about those prayers is that about half the time (at least in our earlier years), the request would catch opposing coaches, players, and families by surprise. Only rarely would an opponent decline. More often than not, they would join us, the players from two teams mixing in together as one and kneeling in reverence to give thanks.

Our players were accustomed to praying after each game. Inside our park, it happened after every game, at every age level. It was just how our teams came to expect that games ended. It wasn't until they started playing outside their own little bubble, they found out what they saw as totally normal didn't even exist in other places. And that's perfectly fine. Kids and adults have that realization every day, in lots of different ways. It's cool that these kids got to see how something they thought was commonplace, others found exceptional. And it's *way* cooler how much it was appreciated by those for whom it was anything but ordinary. In fact, I can't even count the number of times I had a coach or parent from an opposing team tell us, "Thanks for doing that. I really appreciate it."

Here's the point. If you do something often enough, it becomes who you are. That's your *reputation*. In most situations, depending on how well you are known, your reputation precedes you. That is, it gets wherever you're going several steps before you, your words, or your actions do, and it greatly influences how people feel about and treat you.

By the end of most seasons, after you had encountered the same teams more than once, you sort of knew what to expect from playing them. Some had reputations for doing whatever it took to win. Some were known for adult coaches with no qualms about screaming at kids or berating umpires. Others had hyper-involved parents with more energy than self-control. And of course, plenty had good reputations too – teams working hard to do it the right way and those known for developing many high-quality players.

Our reputation? We probably didn't scare anybody. For the most part, we were known for having good kids who competed hard, with good sportsmanship, and who prayed after every game, win or lose. Our teams got noticed in our own way, and that "special" team that went to State was no exception. They didn't win a game at that tournament. But that doesn't mean they came home empty-handed. Not even close. At the end of those tournaments, there's a celebration and trophies for the champions and runners-up. And, as often as is warranted, there is also a Sportsmanship award given to the team best demonstrating that quality during the tournament. In an unexpected, but not unsurprising turn, Matt's team – the one there primarily by grace – was recognized with the State tournament's Sportsmanship Award. It wasn't a championship trophy, but in some ways, it was more meaningful. Maybe not for the 10-year-olds, but the parents couldn't have been prouder of what their boys had accomplished that weekend. And undoubtedly meaningful for the coaches. Part of their job is to protect and strengthen the reputation of the organization they help lead. That job was well done and offered an opportunity for an important lesson. As demonstrated even in how they handled defeat in the regional competition, their reputation was part of what gave them the chance to play at State. From there, they had the same opportunity we all have, in any given situation – to live up to their reputation, or not. They did, and it came with rewards – and, believe it or not, another open door.

Surely that extra weekend of play was the karmic "bonus" for their season, and more than they could have hoped for at the outset, right? Not so fast. In what could be only providential, history repeated itself almost exactly, but on a slightly larger scale. So, what's larger than State? For summer all-star teams in the southern United States, one of the pinnacles of youth baseball is the Dizzy Dean World Series – another invitational tournament held each year in the small town of Southaven, Mississippi. In basically a repeat of our State experience, a qualifying team could not make the trip to Southhaven. That created a void, and an opportunity, for someone else. State directors got requests for candidates, and what do you know, our phone rings again. This time, our coach starts with: "You're not gonna believe this, but...". He was right. It was unbelievable; inconceivable really. The reputation of this little team from Marietta, GA – one not even primarily fueled by its dominance on the field – had once again gained the attention, praise, and recognition of people in a position to reward them. Wow!

I thought I had seen the summit of Matt's joy when we told him they were going to State. It's weird. State was something they could *see*. It was in their grasp but had ultimately slipped through their hands, only to be given back to them by grace. This was something else entirely. This was something beyond the players', or even the parents', imaginations.

Think about it. You get a call on a Sunday night with an invitation for your kid to play in the World Series in two weeks. That's *good* news, right? Mostly. Before that night, you didn't even know this tournament, or the town it's played in, existed. You have 24 hours to decide. Then you (and eleven other families) get to scramble to plan and budget for an impromptu vacation, to Mississippi, in August, when it's routinely 100+ degrees with brutal humidity. There's no other situation on Earth that would create that dynamic, but there we were. Of course, everyone said yes, but it wasn't without sacrifice.

The World Series would begin in two weeks – on the same weekend Carie's parents had planned a family reunion we had already committed to attend. Calling them and explaining that somehow Matt's magical baseball season just refused to end was not something we relished. But we did it. Carie and Liam went to North Carolina to be with family. Matt packed a bag and jumped on a bus with his teammates and coaches bound for Mississippi. My parents and I followed behind. We would attend the tournament for as long as Matt's team stayed alive and join the family reunion, probably a day or so late.

When I tell you that history repeated itself, I wasn't kidding. The Dizzy Dean World Series – though much bigger, hotter, and more spectacular, played out nearly identically on the field to their experience at State. They were guaranteed to play three games, two pool games to build a bracket, and then single elimination after that. They split the first two, getting a chance to taste victory on such a large stage before falling in their first elimination game. Once again, each of those three games ended with a meeting on the mound to pray. Once again, we were joined, and thanked, and apparently noticed. At the end of the tournament, the Mount Paran Spartans were honored with the Sportsmanship Award for the Dizzy Dean World Series. Familiar? Consistent. For better or worse, and it's hard to argue it's not for "better" – that was our reputation. There are a couple of championships in the Mount Paran trophy case, but those sit beside, and some would probably-rightly argue "behind," the two Sportsmanship awards those Spartans brought home from their magical summer run.

As a parent and a coach, I often remind my kids that their name (reputation) is precious. Building and maintaining a good one takes a LOT of consistent behavior, often without consistent recognition. But once recognized, your reputation has power more immense than you can sometimes imagine. Tarnishing a good reputation, especially in today's world of instant gratification and instant access to (good and bad) information, is frighteningly easy. And rehabbing a damaged reputation takes many times more hard work than building it in the first place. "Heroes" with years of acclaim and accomplishment can have those all wiped away by even a single transgression.

Grace is a beautiful thing, and God's is ever-present. In this world, though, the name you build for yourself – in your community, your career, and your relationships – is the most valuable thing you'll ever own. And it's worth protecting with forethought in your words and deeds.

✳✳✳

In the decade I spent on the baseball field with my sons and countless other kids, I encountered many other coaches. Each had their own style, personality, and priorities. As in any other endeavor, leaders must decide what is important to them and develop an approach that attempts to accomplish those goals. Once, during a training clinic, as a very accomplished coach was preparing us for the season ahead, he shared a perspective that has stayed with me to this day.

He said: "Every kid on your team will one day look back on his playing career and will be able to put all of his coaches into one of three categories. They will instantly be able to tell you who their "best or favorite" coach was. And they will be almost as quick to recall their "worst" coach ever. And then, everyone else will sort of fall in the middle – there, but much harder to remember. We're here to make sure you're not the "worst" coach a kid ever has. It's on you to figure out how to be their "best.""

I really like that advice. I didn't take that literally to mean being the best teacher, tactician, or drill sergeant. For me, it was more about trying to be mindful of how each player/child I encountered was different. Each would have their unique talents and tendencies, and I would need to work to figure out how I could adapt my approach to what they brought to the field. That brings us right back to Love Languages, I suppose.

Average or Pretty Great? Yes.

Pretty early on – probably by the third season I coached – I started telling my players and their parents, before we even had a single practice, that I had three goals for my teams. I told them that winning was great and a lot of fun and that if we worked hard and together, we would do plenty of that. But then I gave them a different definition of how I would measure our "success."

My three goals for every team and player I ever coached were these: 1) I want you to have FUN doing this; if you're not, it's not worth the time and effort to be here. To be clear, that doesn't mean EVERYTHING we do is going to be fun all the time – that's not realistic or practical. But we are out here playing a game, so you should enjoy this and WANT to be here. 2) I want you to learn and improve – as individuals and as a team. My job is to help you gain knowledge and develop skills you don't currently have so that by the end of this season, you're better at this than you are today. And perhaps, most importantly... 3) I want you to come back. At the end of this season, I want you to WANT to play baseball again. If we accomplish those three things, regardless of scores or standings, this will be a success.

I know, nobody is running through a brick wall to chase down a championship after *that* pep talk. But it was all true and genuine to what I value. It's probably also why my lifetime winning percentage hovered right around .500, the literal definition of "average" on the field, and why I don't have a mantle jammed with trophies. But it might also be part of the reason baseball has blessed me with more meaningful relationships than I can count and kids who though they haven't seen me on a field in years, still call me "coach." I'll take that.

The biggest reason I'll take it is what I've come to Appreciate about my own sons' experiences with those three rules. Now, remember, they took very different paths. Matt wanted to fly on his own, while Liam preferred to stay closer to the nest. In general, that worked out fine for everyone. And against those three goals I personally had for the experience of baseball, we were routinely checking all the boxes. And then Matt made a decision that changed everything. As he was approaching age 11, he realized he might want something different. He saw many of his friends and teammates jumping out of the recreational league, looking for the higher level of challenge and competition typically found in travel baseball. Carie and I were hesitant, and there was a lot of discussion about if and when that might be the right road to take. Eventually, we relented and told him that if he really wanted to do it, and if he got an invite to join a team based on tryouts, we would support him. He did precisely that and soon was part of a team that included a couple of kids he knew but mostly a whole new cast of characters, including some new coaches. Good for him. Or was it?

I genuinely appreciated the many different coaches Matt had up to that point. Each used their own approach to unlock something else in him that ended up making him a better, more rounded baseball player. But what happens when your newest coach doesn't speak your same "language" at all? You'll recall that while he is plenty self-motivated and driven, Matt's primary Love Language has always been Words of Affirmation. He works hard on his own but truly thrives when others at least notice (and appreciate) the work he puts in to get there.

Unfortunately for him, Matt had landed in a spot where that wasn't going to happen. In fact, his experience was mostly the opposite. From the start, those coaches told him that he was "not right" for the position(s) he had played for years and that he would have to compete to find a spot and get playing time in general.

Now, don't get me wrong, I'm not banging on this organization's approach at all. They are smart people who are very good at what they do. They were, and are, very successful. And there are plenty of kids, and adults, who thrive in environments based on constant pressure, competition, and relative worth. Mostly though, Matt isn't one of them. So, he found himself part of a team whose philosophy was very different from his own. That happens to all of us – in sports, jobs, relationships, etc. We've all looked up and realized, "Wow, this isn't what I thought it would be. This might not be the right place for me." In those situations, you have a few choices: adapt, suffer, or leave.

Matt was 11. He had committed to play for an entire year, so he wasn't leaving. Adaptation proved tricky, too. Unfortunately, his coach's speed in identifying Matt's "wrongness" for certain positions didn't necessarily match his passion for helping Matt develop skills for any other ones.

That leaves suffering. Now, I don't mean that in the potentially dramatic way it might sound. But the truth was, he wasn't having fun – at all. He *was* learning new skills and becoming a more knowledgeable and better-conditioned athlete. But there are those other measures of success. Even though he was so sure of his desires beforehand, the bottom line was that after he got what he "wanted," he didn't really want what he got. Worse, that experience actually broke enough of his spirit and diminished his passion for baseball so much that he wasn't sure he even wanted to play anymore.

Thankfully, with time and distance, that feeling would pass. But for Matt and us, the lesson was learned. For Matt, it became clear that his environment could impact his joy far more than he had realized. Baseball was something he could do lots of ways, in lots of places, but HOW and with WHO he chose to do it suddenly mattered like never before.

Of course, we can't always be in control of our environment, not completely. Sometimes we all end up in groups with values, goals, and approaches different from our own. Being able to appreciate the value of surrounding yourself with people who share your vision of what creates happiness is a valuable skill to develop, and all the better if you can do it at the age of 11.

For me, Matt's experience was a solid reminder of the deal I had made with myself when I decided to coach in the first place. It goes back to those three goals. Having hung up my cleats, I can look back at that time with clarity and know a few things are true. First, I will reiterate that I was an absolutely average coach, measured by wins and losses. But I'll say with equal confidence that while my teams didn't haul in tons of hardware, we did have fun, and we almost always got consistently better. Among the hundreds of kids I've been blessed to work with over the years, I have had a couple of players or parents share that I was their "favorite" coach. That's always nice to hear, of course. What I hope is a better measurement of my "success" is that among those kids, I don't believe there is one who would say I was the reason they hated, didn't enjoy, or didn't want to keep playing baseball. In essence, my approach was baseball's equivalent of the Hippocratic Oath taken by doctors, often encapsulated by the phrase, "First, do no harm."

What if that was the approach we all took in our various endeavors? What if we set three simple goals for our relationships and experiences: Have Fun, Learn and Improve, and Want to Do It Again? And what if our standard for how we treated every person we met, especially those over whom we hold some degree of authority (as a boss, coach, elected official, pastor, etc.) was, "First, do no harm?" We might temper the heights of excellence we could achieve in the absence of such moral guardrails, but what we could stand to "win" might be more than worth it in the end. It has been for me.

Matt would continue to play and ultimately reconnect with the original joy and passion he had for the game he first fell in love with as a curious four-year-old. Whenever that journey eventually ends, I'll be forever grateful for his years in baseball and for the many things they have taught both of us about ourselves and each other.

"That Was Fun. I Love You."

The final story I'll tell in this collection is a poignant complement to the last one. Whereas Matt had to see for himself what exploring new territory looked like and deal with the consequences of those choices, Liam had a very different experience in baseball.

While Matt was ready not to have me as his coach, and honestly flourished as a result, Liam always wanted baseball to be something he and I did together. We're headed straight back to Love Languages. Liam's is Quality Time. For him, the joy of playing is inseparable from his love of being around and involved with other people – and not just me.

From as far back as I can remember, he really cared about WHO else was going to be on his team. In the handful of seasons where he and Matt were together, that always made him happy. Otherwise, it was his friends. On draft days, I would come home with our roster and be excited about the "quality" of the team I had secured. For him, that "quality" was measured by which and how many of his friends he got to play with that season. That's not to say that he didn't take the game seriously or enjoy the actual playing – he did. It's just that he saw a different "big picture."

In this regard, our two sons might be on opposite ends of the spectrum. As the hard-striving, results-oriented kid, Matt could come off the field after winning a championship and still be frustrated that he had struck out that day or made an error in the field. He wouldn't miss the joy entirely, but it might be diminished by his focus on what he thought wasn't quite right. Sound familiar? Apples really do fall close to their trees.

Liam has a different perspective entirely. Perhaps the perfect illustration of this is in his own experience with travel baseball. On the heels of Matt's decision, Carie and I could see the same crossroads in Liam's future. There wasn't a strong league in our park for kids in the 11-12 age group at that time. As Liam and his friends reached that age, many families found themselves in the same boat. By that time, we had played in that league for so long that a core group of kids emerged whose families had a shared interest in finding another solution. As a result, a few of us coaches (Eric, who I introduced to you earlier; another outstanding and successful coach, Ricky; and myself) were approached with the idea of creating a travel team from scratch.

Usually, travel teams form via competitive tryouts. Paid coaches methodically pick a group of players with complementary skills they believe will lead to wins and trophies. For this experience, many parents pay up to several thousands of dollars per year. We took a different approach altogether. Instead of starting with a blank slate and recruiting the best players we could find (kids who probably wouldn't know us or each other), we went the opposite route. We had eleven kids from ten families, who all knew and liked each other and wanted to play together. That might not be how you build a team that consistently wins championships, but it *is* how you create a "family." And when your own kid, and I suspect at least a couple of the others, is fueled by Quality Time, you're probably doing at least something right.

For two straight years, these boys, this baseball "family," hit the travel baseball circuit. We practiced two or three times a week and played all weekend for months straight. That's a LOT of quality time to spend together. Sometimes, we would win; sometimes, we would get killed. Those different outcomes did affect the coaches and some of the parents, but they seemed to have much less impact on the kids themselves. Nobody likes to lose, but regardless of their on-field results, these kids were Having Fun, Learning and Improving, and Wanting to Do It Again – always.

That team formed when Liam and most of his teammates were eleven. The vision was always to keep them together for two solid years with the hope of taking them to Cooperstown, New York, home of Major League Baseball Hall of Fame, and the most coveted 12U baseball tournament in America. Kids from all over the country grow up dreaming of playing there, and each summer, thousands get to realize that dream. For many, it's a "graduation" of sorts from little league baseball. Some will continue to play as teenagers, and some will find the end of their baseball road. In either case, it's a rite of passage we were hoping our boys would get to experience.

In the winter of 2018, as we prepped for the start of our second year together, we learned the Mount Paran Saints had indeed received an invitation to play in Cooperstown. Two years of work on the part of some very dedicated parents had paid off, and our boys would get the opportunity of a once-in-a-lifetime baseball experience. All that remained was to see how they were going to Appreciate it.

If you aren't familiar with the phenomenon that is Cooperstown, let me give you a little context. Each week during every summer, 100+ teams roll through that park for a 6-day blitz that includes a massive opening ceremony parade, a skills competition, and a tournament giving each team at least seven games. It also doubles as a week of summer camp where teams of coaches and their players live together in military style barracks. Through things like group meals, pin trading, and pick-up Whiffle Ball games, they get to meet teams from all around the country. Baseball entirely aside, it's an incredible bonding experience. Players and coaches form memories that last a lifetime. Parents who are coaches and get to have that experience with their own kids are doubly blessed.

Here's the thing about the Cooperstown tournament, though. Of those 100+ teams, they typically fall into one of three groups. Less than a third – maybe 15-20 of them – have a legit chance of winning the whole thing. Many of these teams come with that specific goal in mind – a dangerous proposition, begging for disappointment if you ask me. About a third of the teams are "just happy to be there." They might not win a single game and are there primarily for the experience – perfectly legitimate. The majority fall somewhere in between. They'll win a few, lose a few, and many of their kids will have the awesome experience of hitting a home run on Cooperstown's famously short 200-foot fields.

We knew for sure we weren't in that first group. If we're honest, as coaches, we would probably admit that our boys were tight as a family but maybe a little too loose on the field. We went into that week with modest enough goals, thinking we were probably in the middle group. We had some big, strong kids who likely would hit home runs. We had several solid pitchers. Surely, we would eke out some success. Again, it depends entirely on how you define "success."

That week got off to almost as good a start as it could. In the skills competition, one of our players won the fastest baserunning contest, along with a massive trophy and the nickname "Roadrunner" for the rest of the week. Imagine watching a kid you've known and loved for years take a victory lap around a packed stadium, getting high-fives from hundreds of other kids who are just getting started on one of the best weeks of their lives. That's good stuff and a pretty high "high."

We didn't have to wait long to see what a "low" could look like either. In our first game that next morning, we drew a California team that would end up finishing in the top five. They killed us, blasting multiple home runs and re-introducing us to our old friend, the Mercy Rule. Pretty rough start, but as coaches, we hoped it would be a wake-up call that would kick our boys into a higher gear. Again, if we're honest, in retrospect, our team might not have HAD that many other gears. Some teams are full of aggressive, hard-chargers who stop at nothing to win. Ours was a group of great kids who were good players that loved being together. Thirty minutes after getting creamed on the field, they were back in the barracks telling stories, cracking jokes, and having FUN. Sometimes for adults, (like coaches who wouldn't mind if a beating like that bothered them a little more), that kind of imperviousness can be confusing or even frustrating. Why aren't they mad? Why aren't we working harder to do better? Why don't they CARE? Wait for it...

They DID care; just about something else more. For that group of boys, their collective currency wasn't winning. It was relationships and Quality Time. There's a movie, *Stand By Me*, based on a short story by Stephen King, about the seminal adventures of a group of young boys. The last line of that film is: *"I never had any friends later on, like the ones I had when I was twelve... Jesus.... does anyone?"* That's as good a description you'll find of the spirit of that team. It's also why, despite the relative lack of "wins" on the field, it was the perfect place at the perfect time for Liam.

Though we came close, sadly, the Mount Paran Saints went 0-7 that week in Cooperstown. But that's not necessarily the same thing as going "winless." Every one of those kids had a moment that week that will stay with them for years to come. Some hit their home runs. Some reveled in the challenge of pitching against elite competition. The specific moments may have been different for all of them, but the result was the same: quality time, cemented in their memories.

In the years that have passed since that trip, some of those boys are still among Liam's best friends. To this day, they still gather and tell stories of that week. A while ago, I had the pleasure of overhearing a couple of them talking at a local football game. Inevitably, the topic of Cooperstown came up. One of them said, "I can still remember everything we did, every day that week." Liam's reply? "Yeah, me too. We weren't very good, but that week was the best! I would go there and lose 30 games just to get to do it again." Tell me that's not a "win," or "success;" I'll probably disagree.

I'd be lying if I said that even years later, I don't still think about a few of those games at Cooperstown and how if we had just done one or two little things differently, we probably would have come home with at least one win. For a short while, I actually lost some sleep over stuff like that. There's my cynical brain doing its thing again. *"Dang, it! Why couldn't this have been just a little different or better? This is a lifelong memory; why can't it include at least ONE victory?"* Seriously? Then here comes my wise, sweet, awesome child to give me the answer.

What I wanted to do over, to change for the sake of having a different result that made me feel better, he wanted to do again just for the experience, even if it meant five times as much "failure." Who's the Great Appreciator there, and who still has so much to learn?

Don't get me wrong. I did appreciate Cooperstown in real-time, and even more now. In fact, at the end of that week, I shared a synopsis of our experience with friends and family online.

Revisiting those words now, they seem like the ideal way to close this chapter.

In June of 2019, immediately following that "winless" week, I wrote this:

"I came to Cooperstown with dreams. Like every other dad, I came here hoping to see my son experience wins and home runs. He came close to accomplishing both (blasting a ball three feet from the top of the fence in his first at-bat and playing in several winnable games that ended up not going our way). Disappointing? Sure, a little, but not really. The souvenirs I'm taking home are just as good, if not better. This week, I also saw my son bond with his band of 11 baseball brothers like never before. I saw him celebrate in pure joy alongside his teammates when one of them went yard, and high-five opponents when they did. I got to watch from the dugout and field as he did what he loves most in the game – taking the mound to embrace the lonely challenge of pitching. I watched nervously as he threw five innings, recording strikeouts and giving up some hits but no home runs. I saw my son and his friend carry a hurt teammate arm-in-arm back to the barracks after a deflating come-from-ahead loss. I saw him work with his teammates to decorate his good friend's bunk in those barracks as a surprise for his 13th birthday. I saw my son join his teammates and their various opponents from across the country in prayer around the mound after every game, in genuine thanksgiving just for the chance to play here. I sat with my family in the stands on a beautiful summer night and watched two amazing teams play in the championship game, one winning on a walk-off HR that sent hundreds of kids and parents into a frenzy of joy. And after all our games were finished, on the last day, I got the best souvenir of all. Leaving our team picture, I got a rare minute alone with my boy (who's still a boy with plenty of growing to do, but who became a little more of a man this week). We walked through Dreams Park together, and for the first time that week, he quietly took my hand. A few steps later, he said, *"that was fun; I love you, Dad."* Best

233

souvenir ever from a week I'll remember and treasure forever. Thank you, Cooperstown."

Thank you, Cooperstown, indeed. But even more so, thank you, Liam. My cynical, pessimistic brain tried as hard as it could to get me to see the things I "missed," or "didn't get" in that situation. My 12-year-old son was with me, side-by-side, that whole week. He saw and experienced everything I did, and yet, his takeaway was distilled and beautifully purified into "That was fun. I love you, Dad." How in the world can you NOT Appreciate that? I'll never stop trying.

"As we express our gratitude, we must never forget that the highest appreciation is not to utter words, but to LIVE by them." – *John F. Kennedy*

• **What is your unique Love Language? What about your significant other, or your children?**
  - Recognizing this, how might it be easier to appreciate what others need to hear from you, or how to ask for what you need from them?

• **What is an example of a hidden talent that turned out to be a benefit in your life or in that of others? Did you discover it on your own, or with the help of someone else?**

• **Who are the truly "good people" in your world? Don't wait. Tell them (and their children) today how much you appreciate them.**

• **What is your reputation? Is it the same in all aspects of your life? Why?**

• **What opportunities has your reputation afforded (or cost you)? Why?**

Wisdom to Appreciate:

"Be merciful, even as your Father is merciful." – Luke 6:36

"God's mercy and grace give me hope, for myself, and for our world." – Billy Graham

"But I tell you, do not resist an evil person. If anyone slaps you on the right cheek, turn to them the other cheek also." – Matthew 5:38

Psalm 96:12 – *"Let the field be joyful, and all that is in it."*

Epilogue:

I started this book by declaring that I liked and appreciated its timing. As I reach the finish line and can look back at the experience, and the end product, I realize I do still like and appreciate that, but there's also a lot I discovered that I love.

I love that this book begins with a challenge from one of my children and ends with a declaration from the other – both of which were invitations for me to consider, and then reconsider, my perspective. What happened in between was no less than a miraculous gift – given freely by them and received with gratitude by me.

In these pages, whether you knew me well, or not at all, before reading them, I basically introduced myself to you, the reader. The real gift, though, was the opportunity to meet myself, in a way and on levels I never had previously. I love the idea that it's possible – at 50, or any age, really – to discover aspects of yourself you didn't know existed, and maybe even meet the person others have already known as you for a while now.

I love that my children might read this and find a few of the 'missing pieces' in the puzzle they call Dad. I love that neither of them shares my pessimistic defaults, and how wide open that can make the world for them. And I love the possibility that they – or any of the many young people in my world – through these stories, might discover the power of Appreciation far younger than I ever did.

I love that my parents were still here to see some of this Appreciation - especially for them - dawn on me. It's natural for parents to tell their children how proud they are of them, but somehow less common for children to get, or at least take, the opportunity to reciprocate that gift. I hope these stories help solidify for Bob and Nola how much I love, respect, and appreciate them.

I love that, without it being my intent, this book has given me a vehicle to write letters of love to my children, my parents, my wife, and my friends. And I love that through doing so, my understanding of relationships, in general and specific, has grown exponentially.

Perhaps most of all, I appreciate the evolution in my relationship with God Himself. I spent decades certain I was hearing Him tell me "no." There's a through-line in all of these stories though that tells a different tale. In every instance, through challenges big and small, I've come to realize He was saying, "Wait. That's not what I have for you right now. Look again. There's something better."

In that truth, when I replace the negative space in my head and my heart with gratitude, I see how much more room I have to live a life full of His peace and joy, and in the end... I Can Appreciate That.

And so, dear reader, that brings me to you. I do hope you have found some interest, insight, and even joy in these stories. But much more so, I hope you have found an invitation, and maybe even a path, to join me. As hopefully my story illustrates, it truly is never too late to change the way you think. Adopting a mindset of gratitude and living purposefully in a spirit of Appreciation for the blessings in your life, is a shift with the power to create unbelievable change.

Start with the small stuff. Be mindful of, and on the lookout for, things you can and should appreciate. In no time, you'll probably start seeing them all around you. Some of them will turn out to be so big, you won't believe you've missed them until now. Whatever you find - big or small - SHARE them. Tell people (your spouse, kids, parents, friends, colleagues, whoever) that you appreciate them, and why. And, do it today. That gratitude will spread, slowly at first, but then like fire.

Appreciation is contagious, in a good way; you want to catch it and give it to others.

Start adding **#icanappreciatethat** to your social posts involving special people, places, experiences, or lessons. Over time, you'll be curating a literal collection of appreciation as a reminder to yourself of all your blessings. And, you'll be joining a community of people who share your spirit of gratitude. Trust me; those are the kind of people you want in your world.

Thank you for the opportunity to share what has genuinely been a life-changing experience for me. And thanks for coming along for the ride. There are literally millions of books and stories out there, and you chose this one. I can appreciate that. I hope you will too.

###

Appreciation in Action:

If you're reading this, you've already done something good, whether you knew it or not.

In the spirit of true Appreciation, and "growing what we're given", for every copy of this book sold, a donation will be made to a foundation funding research to fight childhood cancer, in memory of Lake Bozman and his dear friends Mary Elizabeth and Melissa.

For more information and an opportunity to Appreciate this even further, visit www.curechildhoodcancer.org/united today.

About the Author

Steven Crane is the author of the novel *Staring at the Ceiling* and more than a million words of advertising copy throughout his professional writing career. His other full-time jobs are husband and father, with other titles situationally including coach, volunteer, foster parent, mentor, and amateur pancake chef. Steven lives in Marietta, GA, with his wife Carie and their two sons.

Search "I Can Appreciate That" (@ICATstory) on Facebook to join our Community of Gratitude and connect with Appreciators worldwide.

Visit Steven online at: www.brainsofsteel.com

Made in the USA
Columbia, SC
09 September 2021

44461660R00150